AMAZINGLY RIDICULOUS

Dream BIG, Be Ridiculous and Live an Amazing Life

AMAZINGLY RIDICULOUS

Dream BIG, Be Ridiculous
and Live an Amazing Life

Ronald T. Hickey

Featuring
Maurice "The Truth" Willis

Hickey House Books

Sacramento, California

AMAZINGLY RIDICULOUS
Dream BIG, Be Ridiculous and Live an Amazing Life

Copyright ©2018 by Ronald T. Hickey

For Information address: Hickey House Books, 1331 Garden Highway, Sacramento, CA 95833

Printed in the United States of America

10 9 8 7 6 5 4 3 21

ISBN 978-0-9856139-5-2

Editor: Angie D. Carrillo

Hickey House Books
Sacramento, California 95833
www.hickeyhousebooks.com

Library of Congress Cataloging-in-Publication Data

Hickey, Ronald T. (Ronald Terrence), 1964-
    Amazingly Ridiculous: dream big, be ridiculous and live an amazing life /
Ronald T. Hickey
—1st ed.
    p.cm.
    ISBN 978-0-9856139-5-2

Dedication

I first give thanks to God, from which my life flows and who makes all things possible.

To my wife, Ja'Lece, Chloe, and Aterion for being my purpose. My greatest lessons in life flow out of your love for me and from everything you have so courageously taught me about life.

To Maurice "The Truth" Willis, his wife Erica and their children. Your lives have given Amazingly Ridiculous inspiration to me and to this Book, and you are the example for so many other lives.

To my family in East Bakewell, Tennessee, for my strength. The lives you all live have been my every motivation to succeed. I am forever honored to share your blood, your spirit, and your love.

To my deceased mother for bringing me in and making me who I am. She gave me the encouragement to reach for my dreams. Thank you for being true to who you are and teaching me to love myself.

To all of my closest friends, without which this book would not have been possible. Your love, adulation, hopes and dreams are truly what drives me daily to be greater than what I was yesterday. I am eternally grateful for your love and support!

CONTENTS

Live an Amazingly Ridiculous Life

"Bold, Inspirational, and Gigantic dreams have a level of brilliance and a power and a bit of magic in them that almost guarantees that everything you dream of today, tomorrow you can become. So let your dreams be AMAZINGLY RIDICULOUS!"

– Ronald T. Hickey, Author, 12 INSIGHTS

I know Maurice Willis as an incredible young man with talent oozing out of every orifice of his body. To many, Maurice is known as "Reece the Truth." He is my blood relative and 16 years my junior. We are both from a small neighborhood in the small town of East Bakewell, Tennessee. His grandmother and my mother were sisters. Maurice is a phenomenal singer, amazing songwriter, and prolific speaker. The world does not know Maurice as well as it will one day, as he has just begun to *Dream BIG, Be Ridiculous, and Live an Amazing Life.* See, everyone from East Bakewell, TN possesses an amazing array of talent. East Bakewell, TN is an extremely small enclave of Black Americans hidden in the ridges and hostilities of time. The best athletes I have ever seen are from East Bakewell, TN. The greatest singers I have ever heard are from East Bakewell, TN. The greatest artists, thinkers, fathers, mothers, Christians, role models, and good-hearted people I have ever known are from East Bakewell, TN.

For so many Americans, the greatest people we know are from our neighborhoods. I know NFL, NBA, and MLB players and other professional athletes entertain us; just as Hollywood actors, famous music artists, and other celebrities entertain us. However, the truly famous people are in our neighborhoods. The people that really mean something to us grew up right down the street or in the same house as us. But why does talent alone not ensure our success in life? Why does the world not know my cousin Don Allen Johnson, both the greatest basketball player and greatest baseball player I have ever seen? Why does the world not know my brother, Robert Hickey, an absolute athletic phenom and amazing speaker? Why does the world not know, Rodney Johnson, Jeff Johnson, Jarvis Leftwich, Dexter Martin, Darryl Martin, Tracy Willis, Michael Johnson, Rick Rankin, John, Rankin, Elaine Swafford, Larry Moore, Eric Dozier, Joe Ervin, Warrick Tulloss or Pamela Penn, all from my hometown—East Bakewell, TN—and all filled with amazing talent? Why does the world not know Maurice "The Truth" Willis, yet? It is simple. Everyone has talent. Everyone has the ability to be amazing at something. Celebrity athletes, entertainers, and actors do not have a monopoly on talent. Talent alone is not enough. You have to dream big and be willing to do the ridiculous with your amazing talent. You have to be willing to wake up at 4 AM in the morning and not go to bed before midnight. Success comes as a result of the ridiculous things you do when others are sleeping. Greatness rarely occurs between 9 and 5 , Monday - Friday. Your AMAZINGLY RIDICULOUS life happens when you are willing to do the things no one else is willing to do. That level of commitment goes well beyond talent.

At the age of 30-something, after failing at an earlier career in music, after hustling the streets of Chattanooga, after returning to the light of his own truth, Maurice "The Truth" Willis is living an amazing life. His big dreams are now beginning to guide his life; and his ridiculous habits are finally connected to his amazing talents. His life is AMAZINGLY RIDICULOUS! How is Maurice turning his big dreams and ridiculous habits into an amazing life? How is Maurice preparing to come up out of East Bakewell, TN when so many others have not? For most of his life, as far back as 4 or 5 years old, Maurice dreamed of being a great R&B artist. I remember him walking around with a small guitar dressed up in a Michael Jackson costume. He was an outstanding singer, dancer, and song writer early in life. Maurice, like almost every individual from East Bakewell, TN, male and female, was an amazing athlete. He was a star point guard on his Soddy-Daisy

High School basketball team. He was hopeful the NBA was in his future. However, he found himself without any offers of a basketball scholarship from any college or University. So, like many young people, he found himself adjusting his dreams, imagination, and expectations. Maurice turned to his musical talents and the streets of Chattanooga, TN.

I had already left Tennessee 35 years earlier in search of my own success in life when Maurice and I reconnected a few years ago. We had not seen each other in years. Maurice had turned his life over to Christ, restored his belief in his own dreams and was an Ordained Minister in one the largest churches in Chattanooga, TN. After we spoke a few times, I thought Maurice was one of the most amazing young men I had ever met, not because he was my relative, or because he was from the enclave of amazing people from East Bakewell, TN. I thought he was amazing because he walked and talked as a young man that just knew his life was on track to greatness, beyond the ridges and hostilities of time. He was living his dreams and walking in the light of his own truth. He was back to engaging his musical talents. Maurice had become a prolific speaker for the Lord. He was fully engaged in his son's and two daughters' lives. He was out of the streets and being a great husband to his wife. All I could say was, "WOW!" I wondered if what Maurice had could somehow be captured and given to other young people as an example of how to turn their big dreams into an amazing life. I have a 22-year-old son, a 15-year-old daughter, and a daughter in her pre-teens. My wife and I are extremely successful. When my son and our daughters push their dreams out into the universe, their dreams, like all dreams, reflect back. In those reflections, they are not trying to see themselves as their mom or as their dad, despite our successes (I am an author, publisher, business man; and my wife is a Doctor of Pharmacy). Our kids are trying to determine how their generation will receive them and what will be their place here on this earth. My wife and I are too far removed from what our kids imagine for themselves. In the grand scheme of things, they do not want to be like us. Most kids do not grow up and want to be their parents. If we have been good parents, we are able to guide them properly and give them a strong set of principles to live by. But what kids do—they come into contact with those market-driven values, by people they follow—professional athletes, movie stars, or hip hop artists—that influence much greater how they see themselves and how they see their world. When the world finally takes a look at Maurice Willis, they will see a young man that is having the time of his life. That's what I see. How does an overly-talented young man from East Bakewell, TN get to where he is having the time of his life? When my young son and daughters and other young people around the world finally see Maurice Willis, they will see themselves, or at least see a life that they would like to model their lives after—a reasonable and attainable model. We have to stop offering celebrities as role models. They are not connected to our truths. When young people get connected to their truths, they start to reflect their dreams off of the life they imagine living. Reality or not, it becomes their universe to which they start to self-determine their innate worth and their intrinsic reference for happiness. They start to wonder if their big dreams will one day come true, just as the dreams of their favorite idol. Maurice is the manifestation of the very brilliance, power, and magic of bold, inspirational, and gigantic dreams to turn your life into one that is AMAZINGLY RIDICULOUS. Maurice "The Truth" Willis is the perfect example to my son and daughters and millions, perhaps even billions, of other young people around the world that they can turn their big dreams into an amazing life; because Maurice is their neighbor next door or the guy just down the street.

"Dream no small dreams for they have no power to move the hearts of men."

– Johann Wolfgang von Goethe

An amazing life starts with having big dreams and developing ridiculous habits. Small dreams produce a small life. What you dream today determines what you become tomorrow. The bigger your dreams are, the bigger your tomorrow will be. Dreaming turns the power of your creativity on and it connects you to the energy of the universe. The universe truly is your friend and wants you to become everything you imagine becoming. Therefore, you have the innate power to become anything you imagine. So be willing to dream big, be ridiculous, switch your power on, and then go create, as Maurice Willis has, and so many others have, your AMAZINGLY RIDICULOUSLY life.

_____

The Universe is Your Friend

_____

Up until about a few years ago, I had a habit of waking up very early every morning, 4 AM or so. I had a daily routine that I hoped would put my life on a trajectory that would fulfill my big dreams, dreams beyond the small town of East Bakewell, Tennessee. I was dreaming of being a music producer in the Hip Hop industry. Music was my very first love and the primary subject of all of my big dreams. The only problem was, as I would later realize, I was dreaming the wrong dream. Even though, I was a star point guard for my high school, I knew my high school basketball career would one day end. I didn't dream of NBA stardom. I dreamed of the music industry, being like Lil Wayne and T.I. or "Tip." So all during high school, I dreamed of being a great Hip Hop rap artist, lyricist, and song writer. I dreamed I would be a music mogul like Jay Z or Dr. Dre. Yes, it was a big dream! It is still a big dream of mine to have a major impact in the music industry. Music has always been the bedrock of my talents and natural gifts. I actually told friends when we were in high school that I would be a famous musical artist one day. When I am home in East Bakewell, my friends and I still talk about what I said in high school about being a star in the music industry. Although I was not aware at the time, God had even bigger plans. God always has your best interest in mind. So I continued to dream big, and along the way I have found myself having the most AMAZINGLY RIDICULOUS life.

Not everything has worked out as planned. That's life. My first music venture was not successful for me. Others I was associated with were not honest people. Music that I created was stolen from me, and those I helped went on and had some success without acknowledging me. While music has not worked out, there are many other things in my life that have me excited about waking every day. I have an amazing wife that loves me and wonderful children. I am now an ordained minister at one of the largest churches in Chattanooga, TN, and I am excited about expressing myself and my thoughts through this wonderful book, AMAZINGLY RIDICULOUS. Because of my experiences, I know everyone can live an amazing life, even though every detail of your dreams does not materialize. Even when one dream or one hope does not come to fruition, you have to keep dreaming; you have to keep imagining; you have to keep up the hard work; you have to keep the faith that the universe is truly your friend. Each one of us has the power within ourselves to turn our lives into everything we want our lives to be. We simply need to tap into what is already inside. We simply need to act with purpose, commitment, and a big vision. Be ridiculous with your vision, for you really can become all that you imagine. Don't play yourself small. Embrace a righteous set of principles and allow them to take you to a higher destination every day. If you commit to being who you really are and become the person you are really meant to be, your life will be AMAZINGLY RIDICULOUS.

In this book, AMAZINGLY RIDICULOUS, Ron Hickey, my cousin, and I share the character, habits, and principles that we have committed our lives to. I believe if you commit to developing these habits as we have, your life will be everything you dream of and hope for. And remember, life does not come down to one dream or one hope. When one dream does not work out, keep dreaming, just bigger and more boldly. In the end, an amazing life comes down to character and habits, and the principles that are shaped by both. No person is born with character; we have to build character. No person is born with habits; we have to create habits. Stay loyal to what you are, embrace the personal principles presented in this book, build stalwart character, create amazing habits, be ridiculous and your life will be AMAZINGLY RIDICULOUS.

The 19 total letters in the words AMAZINGLY and RIDICULOUS have been used to create words that frame the amazing messages in the 19 AMAZINGLY RIDICULOUS HABITS. Committing to developing the 19 habits described in the book helped me build the character, create the principles, and do the ridiculous things that have led to my big dreams coming true. The 19 words are used as a quick and easy means of memorizing the 19 habits. I believe simplicity is a destination that everyone should seek. These simple action items help simplify the process of developing your best character, forming your greatest habits, and achieving your wildest dreams. The character you develop and the habits you create form the amazing principles that eventually guide your entire life. A devotion to the principles you are able to form moves your life closer and closer to your peak. Your peak is where your life is simplified and you are absolutely everything you can be. Your peak is where you are ridiculous.

Here are the 19 AMAZINGLY RIDICULOUS HABITS that have helped me create an AMAZINGLY RIDICULOUS Life. Commit to developing each – starting today!

Amazingly – First say that you will live life amazingly, and then grow toward the light.

Motion – Stay in constant motion. Travel every day to the very edge of what you know.

Achieve – Achieve to your fullest potential. Come alive, set the world on fire, and give it exactly what it needs.

Zenith – Rise to your Zenith, the highest peak in your life. And live there!

Inspiration – Be Inspired by your dreams. They show

you the possibilities and remind you of your potential. Inspiration is necessary if you are to succeed at truly being You.

Now – Get in the NOW! Get TAPPED IN! Don't tell your Amazingly Ridiculous life to wait.

Gifted – Look within yourself and discover what God has already given you. You already have every gift you need to live an amazing life.

Love – Fall deeply, head-over-heels, in love with yourself. You must love yourself first before you can truly love anyone or anything else.

You – Be You! Believe in You. Be Content with You. Be accepting of You.

Ridiculous – Be Ridiculous! It really is the very ingredient that makes life everything it can be.

Imagination – Your imagination is your art. Become a great artist and let your life be the greatest masterpiece you paint onto the world.

Discovery – Dig into the depths of your own soul. That is where you will discover the real gold. All of the surface stuff is worthless.

Immediacy – Live in the Immediacy of your life. Tomorrow is not a guarantee, and yesterday may hold no real value or no truths today.

Complete – Live a complete three-dimensional life. Become Cubic in the length, width, and height of your life; and accept who you are—completely.

Ultra – Take life to the ultra-limits, then discover what is beyond. Be fearless. Don't play yourself small.

Leap – Take Quantum Leaps when possible, and move with intensity at all times.

Overachieve – Don't be mediocre. Overachieve in all that you do! Overachievement will drive you to nobility; to being impressive, courageous, generous, trustworthy, and at the highest state of self-awareness; all of which, you should want in abundance.

Universe – Force your will upon your world and make the universe bend in your favor.

Switch – Switch the Power On! Be BIG! Be Brilliant! Be Independent! Be Grand! Do not apologize and offer no excuses. Today your life really begins!

I believe most people spend their entire lives searching for success, happiness, harmony, strength, and fulfillment. Those sacred attributes are within, and they derive from the potential power of your brilliance, independence, and grandiosity. You simply have to reach inside and find what is already there and switch your power on. Always believe the Universe is your friend.

"And, when you want something, all the universe conspires in helping you to achieve it."

— Paulo Coelho, The Alchemist

Every single person has dreams, some small, some big. Maybe your dream is to be the best at something in school, in friendship, at work, at a sport, in art, music, or all together some other passion. Sometimes it's hard to keep believing in your dreams. Some dreams die, and at other times your dreams simply remain fantasies or daydreams for a lifetime. If you commit to the 19 AMAZINGLY RIDICULOUS HABITS, develop stalwart character, form great life principles, and truly embrace the thought-provoking messages following each AMAZINGLY RIDICULOUS HABIT in the book, you will quickly see your dreams move closer to becoming your reality. This book is designed to be read easily and over and over and over again. It can be a constant companion that reminds you that the Universe really is your friend and it gives you what you demand with your actions. The "Outro" concludes the book with an ending that explains what it really means to "Dream Big." Your Big Dreams really do lead to an AMAZINGLY RIDICULOUS life.

I believe every person can have an amazing life. So, to assist you in moving toward the light of the vision for your AMAZINGLY RIDICULOUS life, in addition to the 19 AMAZINGLY RIDICULOUS HABITS within the book, I have shared 52 of my favorite, inspiring, empowering, motivating, thought-provoking famous quotes on dreams and success at the very back of the book. I selected 52 quotes so each week of the year a different quote can be read, character can be developed, and habits can be formulated. Enjoy each and meditate on one new quote each week. I hope you find something in this book that inspires you to travel to the moon and back each and every day. And if I happen to see you along the way, during my own trips to the moon and back, I trust and hope you will be living an AMAZINGLY RIDICULOUS Life!

Amazingly

First say that you will live life amazingly, and then grow toward the light.

"We create the outlines of tomorrow with the words we speak today. If I first tell myself that I will live my life amazingly, an image illuminates in my mind; immediately I begin to grow toward the light of the vision."

—Ronald T. Hickey, Author, 12 INSIGHTS

Adversity is a guarantee of life. You will have unfulfilled dreams; people will not like you because of the silliest of reasons; and you will be restricted by circumstance. Life requires you to rely on your determination. Without determination, you cannot create successfully the outlines for your amazing life. During times of uncertainty, challenge and confusion, vision and passion ultimately decide the outcome. Mere doggedness and toughness will not serve you well. You must have an illuminated image of the vision of what you are to become; then you will be determined to grow toward the light. Despite your current circumstances, tell yourself that you will live your life amazingly and watch the very direction your life begins to move in. Observe with true passion and try with all of your might to act with purpose. If you find you are being tested by the situation, simply understand that adversity often requires the consolidation of your resources, energy, and intellect. Take comfort in the fact that you already possess internally everything you need to live amazingly. Adversity is one of God's many tools that He uses to make you stronger, to make you an amazing person.

Be calculated in your actions, and approach each situation without fear and with assuredness, for living an AMAZINGLY RIDICULOUS life requires you to exercise bravery and confidence in your abilities. If your mind is focused and your spirit is energized to the utmost, you will surely grow into the vision you have imagined. Just as the grand tree in the forest had to overcome being hemmed in by other trees and forced to flex its power and strength to grow towards the light, you too must marshal your inner strength and innate power to spread your branches toward the light. When you are finally living an AMAZINGLY RIDICULOUS life, it will be in large part because of the struggles you were brave enough and confident enough to overcome. Having the necessary will, grace, and humility to accept and overcome unfavorable challenges are vital to the development of your inner person, your best character, and your greatest habits. And saying that you will live an amazing life means you are already growing toward the light.

Maurice told me that when he first started to focus on a career in Hip Hop, he, like everyone in the music industry, had dreams of being a superstar, but stardom in the entertainment business is a process that involves painstakingly hard work, ups and downs, setbacks and rip-offs, successes and failures. Getting to where Maurice was early in his songwriting career and where he is currently in life has involved overcoming a great degree of adversity. There is no true success without struggle. There is no superstardom without extreme struggle. Through his early childhood struggles while growing up, he was able to graduate high school without getting into any serious trouble. Even if he was good enough to play college-level basketball, Maurice did not have the grades that would have allowed him to attend a Division I college to play. See, Maurice was born to an unwed teenage mother, my first cousin. His mother never married his father, even though they would eventually have three children together. He has a sister who is thriving, despite her own early childhood struggles, and he has a brother that is in prison. His brother, Norris, named after my own brother, was unable to overcome the valley of despair that life had forced him down into. Through hard work, ups and downs, struggle, despair, sacrifice, and hope, Maurice has been able to hold on to his big dreams and continue to cling to the AMAZINGLY RIDICULOUS habit of first saying he will live an amazing life. Maurice raised his grades just enough to get his high school diploma. His success in life, like most, has not been instant; and where he is today is not where he will be tomorrow. Maurice "The Truth" Willis is still climbing to his greatness. Maurice, with only a high school diploma, moved to Atlanta to give the music industry his best shot. He was young and knew very little about life, and even less about the music industry. He had no money and no place to call his own, but he had a big dream. He also went to Atlanta telling himself that he would live an amazing life. He also had a little help from God. He met some great people along the way that kept him safe and out of trouble. Maurice also met people who took advantage of him. He helped create music that was stolen from him. Those who stole the music went on and had some success without Maurice. That was a hard lesson to learn, but that's life. Those sorts of struggles have made "The Truth" stronger. Those trials and tribulations are what made Maurice, "Reece the Truth." Through the struggles and with painstakingly hard work, vision, and determination, "Reece" kept his wits about himself. He never gave up on himself. Even though Maurice spent years in the streets hustling and working odd jobs, he maintained his big dreams and his commitment to living an amazing life. It is so important not give up on yourself, your hopes, and your dreams. Maurice has found huge success as an ordained minister using his talents on the praise and worship team at his church. His has found his voice and has become a prolific speaker. The more success he comes to know, the more adversity he encounters.

Maurice lost his father to alcohol and his mother has her own crippling addictions to this day. In fact, Maurice lived the majority of his childhood under the care of his grandmothers until both suddenly passed away. Everyone sees the success, but they don't see the true strain of the struggle. There is no really true success without struggle; and great success involves great struggle. I have learned that the greater the success, the greater the adversity can be; for with great dreams of success come great expectations. Great expectations are the touchstones of disappointments.

We dream and expect to be great at many things in life. Maurice has had dreams that have not come true. Each one of us has had unfulfilled dreams. We cannot get down on life because a few things have not worked out. We have to keep telling ourselves that we will live an amazing life. We have had relationships that disappointed us. We have had circumstances in which victory eluded us. These sorts of life-changing disappointments will make you want to quit and question your life decisions. I have had to overcome adversity, after adversity, after adversity in my life. Maurice has had to overcome adversity, after adversity, after adversity in his life. Life can be a serious struggle when things become downright unpleasant at times, but life is also very rewarding if you are able to hang in there and meet your challenges with mental toughness, bravery, goodwill, stalwart character, passion, and big dreams. In life, not everything works out, not everyone will like you, and not everyone will find favor in your flavor. You can't please everyone, and there will always be adversity at every level as you rise. What defines you as a human is how you handle that adversity, how you deal with disappointment. Bob Marley once said, *"The Truth is, everyone is going to hurt you. You just got to find the ones worth struggling for."* The struggle is real, but so is the victory. You first have to tell yourself that you will live amazingly.

One area I continue to grow in myself is in an understanding that no matter how tough life may get from time to time, no matter the challenges I am faced with, I have to see my life as amazing, irrespective of what someone else thinks. I have a better understanding of my adversity. I now see adversity as the fertilizer that has helped me grow into the amazing spirit that I am. Without those struggles, I would not be who I am. Without the struggle, Maurice would not be who is he. Without the struggle, you would not be you. The first thing I had to say to myself is, "I am worth struggling for!" The first thing you have to say to yourself is, "I am worth struggling for!" Your life is amazing when you realize it is worth your own struggles. The music and entertainment industries, professional sports leagues, living a life in public view, celebrity lives and the more normal lives of teachers, doctors, bus drivers, salon owner and others are really challenging places to make an amazing life, without casting yourself in the images of others' expectations. Lives lived in public environments and on social media have a way of causing you to lose your self-identity. But you cannot let the public dictate your happiness or how you feel about yourself.

Life rarely goes the way we plan. Despite that, we have to hold on to the will to dream and believe our lives are meant to be amazing. We have to realize how blessed we truly are and appreciate where we are. We have to recite, "I AM ENOUGH." Loving oneself helps one move closer to understanding that no matter the outcome of a particular experience in life, one must walk in the light of one's own truth at all times. We must tell ourselves that we are worth the struggle. I must tell myself I will live amazingly. "I AM ENOUGH, and MY ENOUGH is AMAZINGLY RIDICULOUS!" You must say the same. As long as we know the truth about ourselves, continue to run the marathon with grace and determination, and allow adversity to water and fertilize our paths and refuse to be knocked down for too long, God will cause the universe to surrender to our will. First say you will live amazingly and then let your actions produce an AMAZINGLY RIDICULOUS life.

2ND HABIT

_____

Motion

_____

Stay in constant motion. Travel every day to the very edge of what you know.

"No man is great enough or wise enough for any of us to surrender our destiny to. The only way in which anyone can lead us is to restore in us the belief in our own guidance."

—Henry Miller, Author

To live an AMAZINGLY RIDICULOUS life, you must grow beyond your self-imposed limits and restore your belief in your passion, purpose, and big dreams to guide your life. It is our big dreams that move us to the very edge of what we believe we know and allows us to grow. Your personal growth is all based on your movement beyond what you think you know. One must not surrender his or her destiny to another person, and we must move constantly and grow toward our own light. We should seek constant growth in the belief in our own guidance. To grow constantly requires constant movement. You must keep your life in motion at all times, for there is no point in your life when you should give up growing your belief in yourself. When growth stops, decline begins. Flowing water remains fresh, and only the constant rotation of the earth creates night and day. Every aspect of your personality—mind, body and spirit—have one particular quality in common, that is exercise causes them to grow. Thus, lack of exercise will cause them to become stagnate. Therefore, you must commit to the exertion of constant movement to grow an AMAZINGLY RIDICULOUS life. You have to put some great effort into becoming amazing. A ridiculous effort produces ridiculous results. No one can do this for you. Surrender your destiny to no one. You get out of your life exactly what you put into your life. If you sit and watch television or play on the computer all day and never exercise, your body will decline quickly. You must get up, get out and exercise to keep the body strong. Exercising is exerting energy. If you don't exert energy, you will not grow. You get out what you put in–NINO: *Nothing In Nothing Out*. That is why, no matter how old or how young you are, no matter how much you have accomplished, you must keep all aspects of your life in motion. The exertion of any energy—whether physical, emotional, mental or spiritual—is movement. Movement is growth. Growth leads to an AMAZINGLY RIDICULOUS life!

When a professional athlete retires, he or she knows that they cannot stop moving. Much of life is still ahead of them, because in most cases they retire at a young age, in comparison to the normal retirement age of 65. But their bodies feel much older than their actual age because of what professional athletes have to put their bodies through to perform at the elite athletic level. That's life for professional athlete. Their bodies get banged up. Because their bodies are aged beyond their years, they know that even in retirement they need to keep exercising 3 to 4 days each week. If a retired professional athlete does not exercise, the constant trauma their bodies have experienced would catch up with them quickly. So exercising and staying in physical motion is critical to their health. I use professional athletes as an example because so many of us watch them perform year after year. Watching sporting events is a primary form of entertainment in this country. But the human mind is similar to the human body. It must be exercised. As we develop the mind we must exercise it daily, even when we reach a mature age. I read constantly, and I read as many books as possible. I read to this day nonstop. I am trying to learn everything I possibly can. I exercise my body and work on expanding my mind and feeding my soul each day. You grow only when your body, mind, and spirit are exercised daily. Muscles grow when they work against the resistance caused by exercise. Mental faculties sharpen when the mind is engaged in critical thinking. The spirit soars joyously to the moon and back when some endeavor you have undertaken excites it. Your spirit begs for excitement. Keeping the spirit excited requires great effort, but if you do not keep your spirit in constant motion you will fall from your mental and emtional heights very quickly. Just like a professional athlete must keep his or her body in motion to remain agile and vibrant, we too must keep moving to remain vibrant and healthy. Likewise, if you do not keep your life moving upward you will fall from the heights of happiness, self-love, and amazement very quickly. You must exercise your mind with the same intensity that an athlete exercises his body. Daily physical exertions, varied mental interests, and exciting adventures to keep your muscles exercised, the mind invigorated, and the soul excited; respectively, are essential to growing physical vitality, mental strength, and spiritual stamina for your life. So move and grow! Your life depends on you doing so.

When you consider the life of Maurice "The Truth" Willis, what you may observe on the outside is the son of an unwed teenage mother, a man that is under-educated, a man raised by his grandparents, or a man gifted with amazing talent; but not quite living up to his talents. Maurice was considered slightly undersized for a career as a basketball player, even though he had great athletic skills. The world can measure his physical size and maybe even observe the outer-most struggles of his life, but no one in the world can, with any degree of accuracy, measure his heart. No one in the world can observe the movements in his mind and spirit. The world can measure his speed, as he has gotten slower as he has matured, but the world cannot put a stop watch to his mental toughness. Everyone could watch Maurice play basketball, sing a song he had written, or struggle on an exam in school, but no one could imagine his determination to become better and better each year to become the best man he possibly can be. I don't know if Maurice "The Truth" Willis has become the best man he can be yet, but I do know that no one is now saying that he is undersized. In fact, in many aspects of life, Maurice has become the prototype for the millennial generation; because he has kept his life in motion. Millennials face many challenges that previous generations did not experience. Adversity does its best to stop you from growing. When his music was stolen, Maurice did not quit. He still sings and writes songs. He did not quit because he was marginally educated. Maurice reads constantly now to sharpen his mind. His spirit has grown so large that he consumes an entire room when he walks in. That's growth! That's movement! Every year Maurice becomes stronger, faster, and smarter. Your education has to be a lifetime commitment. Read and learn. Your growth in life has to be a daily focus. Move beyond all resistance. Place no arbitrary limits on your life. Stay in motion to increase your spiritual agility, emotional endurance, and mental toughness for the game of life. Like Maurice, you must move through struggles, shortcomings, disappointments, and injuries. Give all that you have to life; every single minute, every single action, every single day—until you have nothing else to give. Become the best you possibly can be by keeping your mind, body, and spirit in constant motion. To become the best you possible, you have to exercise the very essence of who you are. Each day, I work with intensity at being my absolute best. Each day, Maurice works with intensity at being his absolute best. Your work is what others will see in you. Your work is what will take you to the destinations you seek. Work is movement, and movement is growth. Stay in motion.

You cannot reverse the effects of time on your body, mind, and spirit, but you can slow the speed at which time takes its toll. Life is not an easy proposition; in fact, life is overwhelming and difficult at times, but the more you grow the more prepared you will be to take on life's many challenges when they come your way. Get ready and stay ready. Living an AMAZINGLY RIDICULOUS life will requires you to be your very best at all times, increase your inner strength continuously, and ward off the infirmities of time. So stay in constant motion, and travel to the moon and back every day. Your mind, body, and soul needs the exercise to keep growing into the best you can be. Remaining stagnant in any aspect of your life can be the very kryptonite to your Super-Manhood or Super-Womanhood. That's why Maurice and I are constantly pushing to find ways to grow mentally, physically, and spiritually. The Great Muhammad Ali once wrote, *"If at 50, I thought as I did when I was 20, then I would have wasted 30 years of my life."* That is the goal, to look over your life and see that you have steadily and constantly gotten better each year, year after year. Never remain stagnant. If 20 years from now, your mental capacity and spiritual aware-ness remain as they are at your current age, then you will have wasted 20 years of your life. Maurice knows if he wants to become a great person in any aspect, he has to continue to educate himself and grow his un-derstanding. Your abilities in life become stronger only after you have practiced, practiced, practiced. Life as an athlete, a musician, an artist, a doctor, an attorney, a police officer, a writer, or anything else one wants to be in life requires one to practice to get better. Practice is motion, and motion in growing. There is no book we can study to learn everything we need to know about life. You can only live and learn as you go. There's no right or wrong in living, just truth. The truth of living is what excites my mind and keeps my soul passionate about the life ahead of me. Everyone must find their own spark. What excites your soul about your life or your areas of interest? To stay in motion, you must wake every day excited about your life. If you are excited, you will grow. The more you grow, the more you'll find truth. The more you find truth, the more you'll be able to relate and understand others and this life we live. Once you begin to understand life with a much greater degree of passion and purpose, the more you will be able to create an AMAZINGLY RIDICULOUS life for yourself.

I watch as Maurice lives his life with so much passion, vision and purpose. He gives his wife, children, family, friends and God everything he has to give; and it allows him to travel to the moon and back each day as he chases his big dreams. He is excited about his life, more than he has ever been. His life is no less complicated than the next person's; but the geometry of his life, the competition in the valley, and the strategies to win are all intrinsic elements of his daily life that keep him excited. Maurice is trying to figure out what direction his life needs to move in next. Trying to figure out the next right move keeps his mind and spirit in constant motion; therefore, he is moving and grow-ing closer to his truth, closer to the edges of what he knows. Traveling to the moon and back is moving each day to the very edge of what you know about yourself. You should surrender your destiny to no one, and your constant motion should keep you so excited about your life and at the very edge of what you know about yourself. It's at this edge of knowledge from which you grow. Believe in the guidance of your own big dreams. Get excited about where your constant motion allows you to travel to. So do as Maurice and I have done; fol-low your wildest dreams and love what you do, and do what you love. Do every single day better than you did it yesterday, and when you start to take your daily trips to the edge of what you know about yourself, stop to see just how far you have traveled every now and again and look at just how amazing you have become. Then quickly get it all back in MOTION!

3RD HABIT

Achieve

Achieve to your fullest potential. Come alive, set the world on fire and give it exactly what it needs.

"Don't ask yourself what the world needs, ask yourself what makes you come alive. And then go and do that. Because what the world needs is people who have come alive."

— Howard Washington Thurman

You have surely heard before that the mind is a powerful energy source, and you can achieve anything you put your mind to. Your soul is a powerful energy source as well. The human mind is a physical object, the brain; it generates mental energy. The human soul is a metaphysical—nevertheless real—object that generates spiritual energy. The mind and the soul together create an unfathomable tangle of wires and dense webs through which your mental and spiritual energy flows. The human mind and its soul is a massive energy source that creates all of your emotions, memories, instincts, actions, reactions, and thoughts. Whatever the mind conjures up enters into its channel of awareness and flows down to the soul's reservoir. Your soul's reservoir is metaphorically likened to an enormous tank of flammable liquid. When you have thoughts of achievements, a spark is generated that zooms down your mind's channel of tangled strands at a speed faster than the speed of light. When that small spark reaches your reservoir, it sets your tank on fire. But in your mind and soul, there are far more strands with no sparks zooming through them than there are strands carrying sparks from your emotions, memories, instincts, actions, reactions, and thoughts. Most of the space in your reservoir is not energized; it is unused, and nearly lifeless from lack of brain activity due to too much television and social media and too little energizing mental stimulation. Most people live their entire life and use very little of their brain's potential power. No wonder the majority of people do not reach their full potential and live life as underachievers. You must make these dormant areas of your mind and soul come alive. You must set them ablaze and turn them into a burning inferno. The energy generated from the fire will heat up your mind with exciting thoughts, burn your soul with fervent desire, and propel you at the speed of light to your fullest potential. You will achieve beyond your wildest dreams, and in the process, you will give the world exactly what it needs—a soul that has come alive and is on fire.

With passionate thoughts, strong emotions, and determined actions, you can generate activity in the mind's central core. This space is like a vibrant stream; when activated, its energy flows into the fueled reservoir of your soul. Your mental energy can rekindle spiritual sparks in the inactive areas of your mind and soul, and in the river that connects the two, and set them ablaze. This blaze is ignited by your mental energy. Your spiritual energy rejuvenates the soul, which makes personal achievements beyond your normal mental abilities very possible. This is precisely what I experience each day as I mediate and fill my mind with knowledge. My many mental thoughts excite my spirit and send a spark down to my soul. I am excited about the life that is in front of me. I can hardly wait to see what more I will achieve with my life. Without the soul being set on fire, reaching your full potential is impossible. You have to want something so badly that the thought of achieving it sends a spark from your brain down to the flammable liquid in the reservoir in your soul and sets your whole spirit on fire. You have to be on fire to live an AMAZINGLY RIDICULOUS life. When we watch Serena Williams win a Grand Slam, our favorite NFL team win the Superbowl, or our favorite actor perform an Oscar-winning role, that's because their souls are on fire. That is precisely why they are able to perform at the highest level of achievement. That is why an artist wins the album of the year or an NFL player wins Rookie Player of the Year. That's why NBA teams win championships and Olympians win gold medals–AMAZINGLY RIDICULOUS! Come alive and live your life to the fullest! Light a living fire in your soul and keep it burning until you have achieved all that your heart desires, at the highest level of achievement.

Once you come alive and set your soul ablaze, your fire will cause others around you to come alive. Life is not simply a physical experience. We are also spiritual beings with the ability to infect others with our energy. A spark in you can create a fire in a friend, a family member, your mom, your dad, in someone you barely know, or your teammate. I am an author and publisher. I am from the small town of East Bakewell, Tennessee. I am also a born leader. My name, Ronald, is Celtic, meaning "decision maker, ruler, King." I build winning attitudes in others around me and inspire them to be their very best. When I am at my very best, everyone around me is at their best. My spark creates sparks in others. My spark has given Maurice the spark he needs to become the champion he is destined to become. Likewise, Maurice will create sparks in those around him. If we keep creating these sparks we can set the human race on fire and cure some of our most critical human issues. Humans really are spiritually connected. And when a group of people come alive and their souls are set on fire, lives change, families move up to the upper room, neighborhoods thrive, the world dances to a new rhythm of life, and yes, teams win sports championships—all because of just one spark from you. You have the power to generate great achievements in yourself, in others around you, and in the world. The world needs you to come alive.

Maurice tells me that he incessantly tries to find ways to achieve to his fullest potential. He worked hard to become the best Hip Hop artist he could. While that has not worked out, he now works equally as hard to become the best person, best husband, best father, best friend, and best man of God he can be. He has set his soul on fire so he can become the best speaker, worship leader, co-worker, and writer. Maurice understands that his fire can spark an achievement in his wife, children, brother, sister, friends or someone else. His success is his family's success. His success is East Bakewell, Tennessee's success. We achieve, not only for ourselves, but so others around us can achieve as well. After all, success can be a lonely place if you are the only one sitting at the top. That's why I am constantly reading and meditating to find my truth so I can become a better spirit; encouraging my family, friends and folks in Tennessee and elsewhere that are still in the struggle; encouraging my family and business colleagues to join me in achieving great success. As humans, we relished the relationship we develop with other highly successful people. Successful people produce other successful people. Consider this book. Three men from the same small community in Tennessee have come together to write and publish a book. I am the author and publisher. Maurice has co-authored parts of the book and lent his life stories, and Joe Ervin provided the professional images for the book cover and the book's website. We have lit a fire in each other. This work will light a fire in the lives of those around the world who read this book and in others from our neighborhood and surrounding communities. This is the power of the human spirit when we ignite a fire in others with a spark of encouragement, a spark of love, a spark of brotherhood and sisterhood. It's these invisible but passionate relationships that made a world of difference in our lives. We can learn so much about ourselves and become a better person each year due to the many valuable relationships with other successful people. Remember, success produces success. Sparks produce flames. We are sparking a fire in the world.

I have achieved great success in life because of the spark of others. I have created great success in others' lives because I sparked their success. It can be a great coach who puts a spark in us, great teammates who put a spark in us, or great friends who put a spark in us; and you can put a spark in all of them. Great achievements create other great achievements. I believe that if I achieve, then everyone around me will achieve in same measure. All humans are that interconnected in life. Even when life has not worked out the way we planned it, there can be nothing but excitement in finding out how my life will eventually turn out. Maurice says he is excited about his future because he is excited about his life. All of the sparks flying around will surely cause a huge human blaze. That is exactly what made his life AMAZINGLY RIDICULOUS. Therefore, Maurice knows he will achieve something of great measure. Set your soul on fire and aim high! Failure to aim high, not failure itself, is the great sin. We can achieve greatly even when it appears that we have failed at something. There are no rules to becoming a great athlete, a great police officer, a great nurse, a great teacher or a great street sweeper; you just have to go out and do it greatly and with all your might. There is no set road map for achieving stardom, becoming a great wife or husband, or creating a spark in others. You just have to stay focused on achieving and giving the world exactly what it needs—you on fire!

Maurice "The Truth" Willis says it this way, "To achieve greatly you definitely need great energy around you, other beautiful souls who keep your spirit up. In order to achieve greatly, you have to walk in the light of your own fire and keep loved ones around you who also keep it truthful with you at all times—no sugar-coated cotton candy type of people. You need friends who can critique out of love and tell you the things that others will not. That's my spiritual connection with my family, friends, and loved ones. They keep it real with me and push me to keep my fire burning. And of course, I maintain a close connection with God, for God is my true spark in life. I find favor in God's will, and I allow God to find favor in my actions. The ultimate achievement in life is becoming everything God wills you to become. Everyone has an opinion on what you should be in life, but God holds the key to every door you will ever try to open. You have to grab the keys to your AMAZINGLY RIDICULOUS life from His outstretched hands. Then come alive and achieve to your fullest potential."

4TH HABIT

Zenith

Rise to your Zenith, the highest peak in your life. And live there!

"Hiding, secrets, and not being able to be yourself is one of the worst things ever for a person. It gives you low self-esteem. You never get to reach that peak in your life. You should always be able to be yourself and be proud of yourself."

—Grace Jones

You must navigate your life toward a single highest peak, and live there. There are a number of processes by which to achieve this, from educating yourself, to using your creative imagination, to adopting mind-centering methods. Whatever method you incorporate, the intent is to move your life to the single highest point of personal self-esteem—where you can be yourself and be proud of yourself. This is the one place in life where you can come out from your hiding place and abandon your secrets. Your peak is the point upon which your life is truly defined by you.

Your peak determines your outlook on life. It helps you develop your points of view.

Your peak is the center of your life. It is the very point from which your perspectives develop.

Your peak is a destination that provides your life a point to navigate to.

Your peak is the essence of your life. It is the point that you attempt to get others to see in you.

Your peak determines the height of your achievements. It is your point of reference.

Your peak is a defined point in this world. It is a point at which you are miniscule and shapeless.

Your peak is your actual arrival and your departure. It marks your movement in time.

Your peak is your solitary space. It is the point where no one else matters.

Your peak is where you go to be yourself. It is the point that measures your self-worth.

Once you reach your peak in self-love and self-determination, your life takes on the above attributes and descriptions. To the contrary, a life that has not reached its peak and has no focal point for self-grandiosity is a life hidden from plain view; in fact, you may be hiding from yourself. You cannot live an AMAZINGLY RIDICULOUS life if you spread yourself over the many opinions of others. You cannot approach the peak in self-esteem if you're engaged in random activities of the heart and mind. Life has to have a focus if you are to love yourself and be proud of the person you have become. Your mental and spiritual energies must be concentrated at a centralized point so your energies can generate the necessary power to move you toward your peak. Your energies have the demands of fifty thousand influences and are easily drained if used for supporting aimless wanderings. Wandering leads to self-debilitating feelings such as self-hatred, confusion, low self-esteem, ignorance, unhappiness, and helplessness. When your life is steadfastly moving toward its peak, however, you expend your energies on just a few focused things. Your mind is freed from the fifty thousand distractions, and your life loaves in shear harmony with the universe. To state without exaggeration, the world revolves around you when you are at your peak. You no longer have to waste time and energy chasing success, happiness, and fortune; those things will constantly surround you. Your AMAZINGLY RIDICULOUS life will simply appear before you. Get to that point, and live there!

I have always refused to compare myself to others—their careers, their successes, their happiness, their looks, their money, or their lives. We live in a time when comparisons are normal and natural. We love to compare the size of our homes and brag about who has the biggest house. We compare cell phones then debate who has the latest and the greatest phone. We compare new car models to old car models. We talk about home run hitters to argue who was the best MLB hitter of all times. We compare NFL teams, running backs and quarterbacks to argue who is or was the best. We compare our fashion attire to see who is wearing the "dope" gear. It is extremely difficult to do anything in life and escape being compared to someone else. And to be honest, most buying decisions are made based on what others will think; whether we are buying jeans, a phone, sunglasses, a car, a home, a television, or something else. We love to "floss", "slay", and show off some "bling." We love to flex our muscles and show off how much money we have, but another person's life is not our life. Another person's career in music, sports, or Hollywood is not the same as anyone else's career. My best friend's success is not mine. One person's happiness is not another person's happiness. One person's sadness is not another person's sadness. The looks of one fashion model are not the looks of any other model. My success is my success; my failures are my failures, no one else's.

Maurice "The Truth" said that this is the very reason he never ran with the "in crowd." He said his life has always been about rising to his own peak in life.

Maurice's life is Maurice's life. My life is my life, and your life is your life. Comparing his life, your life or my life to someone else's serves no meaningful purpose. When we refuse to compare ourselves to others, we immediately started to rise to our own Zenith. You can't be you if you are wandering in a notion of comparing yourself to others. The weight of others' opinions is the very device that holds you down and prevents you from rising to your peak. Maurice said, "When I came to the realization that, at the end of the day, I can only be the best me, that's when I reached my peak." We have good friends that are also professional artists in the music industry. We have friends that are great at many other things in life. Maurice had to remain true to himself and chart his own path. That's why he has found himself writing and singing the Lord's music. He is not out in the streets working to become a great R&B or Hip Hop artist. Success in R&B and Hip Hop is someone else's success, not his. Maurice has just released a series of AMAZINGLY RIDICULOUS inspirational songs on social media, *Calling on His Name* and *Owe It All to You*. Maurice's success in music and writing is meant to be his success, no one else's. His level of ability is different from any other. My level of ability and your level of ability are different from all others. Everyone has the ability to be great! Everyone has their own level of talent. Everyone has their own peak. As soon as we realize that our lives are our lives to live, then we can focus on being the best at whatever it is we are here to do in this life. If you are a bricklayer, rise to your zenith and live there. If you are a train conductor, reach your peak and be the best train conductor you can be.

If you are a student in school or college, become the best student you possibly can. Don't try to be like me, Mike, LeBron, Steve, Peter, or Paul. Be yourself. Rise to your zenith, and live there.

Nothing in life lasts forever. Everything comes to an end. We can't sugarcoat that truth. Many people expect to be around for a long time. Some do, and some don't. Reach your peak as soon as you can and live there. Let God give the increase to longevity. "The Truth" told me that he gives everything he has to each and every song, every word, and every thought; even in the shower. That's RIDICULOUS! Maurice said, "I told myself from the very beginning that my time would be up the very day I felt that I couldn't give my very best and sing and write at my peak. When that day comes, I will say goodbye gracefully." Have you ever seen an artist who hung around too long? I remember going to a Whitney Houston concert in Las Vegas during her last tour. The concert in Vegas was fabulous. The next weekend, she was in Oakland, and she couldn't quite hit the notes likes she once could, and the tour came to an abrupt end. When you are at your peak at anything, you know the very moment when you are unable to remain at your peak. That becomes the exact moment when your performance starts to decline. In maturity, I am no longer at my peak physically; but I am still rising as a writer and publisher. Maurice is still rising as an artist, song writer, producer, speaker, and man of God. When you reach your Zenith, your mind has to stay there. As you reach the peak in one aspect of your life, look for another peak in your life and live there. Your peak will be that place where you live an AMAZINGLY

RIDICULOUS life! Your peak is where you will find your truth.

My truth is my peak. My truth is the destination that provides my life a point to navigate to. My truth is the essence of my life. It is the point that I attempt to get others to see in me. My truth determines the height of my achievements. It is my point of reference for my success. My truth is a defined point in my life. It is a point at which I am miniscule and shapeless. My truth is my actual arrival and my departure. It marks my movement in time. My truth is my solitary space. It is the point where no one else matters. My truth is where I go to be myself. It is the point where I measure my own self-worth.

What is your peak? What is the destination that provides your life a point to navigate to? What is the true essence of your life? What is the point that you attempt to get others to see in you? What determines the height of your achievements? What is your point of reference for your success? What is a defined point in your life—the point at which you are very miniscule and shapeless? What are your actual arrival and your departure—the points that mark your movement in time? What is your solitary space—the place where no one else matters? What is the place where you go to be yourself—the point where you measure your own self-worth? If your peak is being a nurse, doctor, poet, electrician, plumber, mother, brother, uncle, aunt, bus driver, sister, father, dancer, pianist, artist, architect, engineer, scientist, actor, professional athlete or something else, then rise to the zenith of your life, and live there. Your peak is the very place where your life will be AMAZINGLY RIDICULOUS, and you will be proud of yourself and free.

5TH HABIT

Inspiration

Be Inspired by your dreams. They show you the possibilities and remind you of your true potential. Inspiration is necessary if you are to succeed at being You.

"Consult not your fears but your hopes and your dreams. Think not about your frustrations, but about your unfulfilled potential. Concern yourself not with what you tried and failed in, but with what it is still possible for you to do."

—Pope John XXIII

Your hopes and dreams should be your constant companions. They should be the inspiration that drives your every action. Your mind needs an image, a dream, an inspiration to focus on for the mind and soul to function productively. Your dreams are absolutely who you are becoming. They connect with your everyday outward images of life to make you whole. Sight, sound, touch, taste, and smell are the five outer senses that transport the images of your mind into thought and action. There are no actions without thought. There are no thoughts without images–the mental outputs of the senses. This is precisely why you should never consult your fears, frustrations, or failures. Your negative thoughts, connected to negative images, will produce negative actions. When you dream big, those powerful positive images create amazing thoughts that lead to amazing actions. Your AMAZINGLY RIDICULOUS life begins with your AMAZINGLY RIDICULOUS images produced by your AMAZINGLY RIDICULOUS dreams. Be inspired by your hopes and your dreams!

In dreaming, you seek an absolute connection with the spiritual. The spiritual is a place of beauty that you love to escape to. It inspires you to see the best in yourself and the best in others. But life is relative; therefore, the absolute can only exist in your mind. Your spiritual place of beauty is a place you cannot remain forever, for eventually you have to wake up to the realities of life. What you can do is bring forth from your imaginary place the inspiration of your images, hopes and dreams; encouraging you to return often. They encourage you to achieve beyond your limits, beyond your obstacles, beyond yourself. Inspiration is to your life what sunshine is to a flower. Without it you will never become as beautiful as you can possibly be. As Pope John XXIII suggested, *"...concern yourself with what it is still possible for you to do."* You cannot possibly understand what is possible if you are not allowing yourself to be inspired by your dreams. Inspiration is your sunshine.

Seeking your full potential may be one of your greatest goals. Part of reaching such a goal is you must navigate every path that appears before you. You should learn every skill that you wish to master. You must experiment with every curiosity that excites your senses. You should work to overcome every insecurity, doubt, and uncertainty. You should engage your every interest on your every path in life. Eliminate your every obstacle, and then you will learn that your dreams and your reality converge at a particular vertex, an absolute space in time, connecting your human interests with your spiritual aspirations. This is where lofty contemplations of your imagination meet the active living of your mundane soul. This is the place where you discover what is still possible for you to do. This is the place of your hopes and your dreams. This is the place where you first imagine your AMAZINGLY RIDICULOUS life.

Inspiration has many sources external to the soul. Inspiration can come from a song, a speech, a movie, a word from a dear friend, a poem, a parent, or a number of other things that exist outside of you. While we are inspired by things outside of us, our greatest source of inspiration comes from within. For most, our mothers, fathers, teachers, coaches, family, and friends may inspire us to be the best and make us believe we can be anything we want to be in life; but it is our own big dreams that have inspired us the most. I remember Maurice sharing with me that everyone thought he was crazy when he said he was moving to Atlanta to become a major player in the music industry. Maurice had very little money and had never lived away from home, but his big dreams gave him the vision of what was possible for him to do. Maurice said, "When I was deciding what I would do with my life and after I realized that being a player in the NBA was not in my future, I did not consult my fears, frustrations, or failures. I consulted only my hopes and my dreams." It would have been so easy for Maurice to allow his fears to talk himself out of moving to Atlanta. Maurice, within a very short period of time, lost is father, both grandmothers, and one of his grandfathers. His entire support system was gone in the blink of an eye. While his mother is still alive, she was never a significant contributor to his life. Seventeen years later, Maurice is living proof of what your life can be if you are willing to become inspired by your own dreams. Maurice is not exactly where he wants to be, but he is on his way. His big dreams led him to Atlanta, and now he is back in Chattanooga, TN. The lessons he has learned along the way have taught and inspired him to do the things he is doing today and have given him the confidence to believe that all he dreams of will come true. This book is one of those dreams coming true. And your dreams will come true as well if you are willing to be inspired by them. Where are you willing to allow your dreams, not your fears, to lead you? Have you been dreaming of moving to Atlanta, Los Angeles, Chicago, New York or somewhere else? Have you been thinking about going back to school, training for a new job, getting your own place, or something else? We have to audition for roles we want to play in life. The audition begins in our hopes and dreams. While life does not give us every role we audition for, we must be willing to be inspired, not frustrated, by the process of trying again and again until we are successful. You should not concern yourself with what you have failed at, but concern yourself with what you believe you still have the ability to do. Learn from your failures, as Maurice has, as I have, as countless other people have, and apply the lessons in your next dream. The fact is, in life we are turned down more times than we actually get the role we want. Not all dreams come true. Is this frustrating? Does this eat at your soul? Does it make you feel like a failure at times? Absolutely! But you must continue to have big dreams, and they will not allow you to focus on the roles in life that you do not get. Focus only on the roles that you have gotten; your successes, your happiness, your joys, and your triumphs. Focus on the dreams that can still come true and the roles you will get. Maurice says, "I do not allow the memories of past failures, frustrations, or fears hold me back. Because I know there will be other successes, I dream big, and I am inspired to become a better songwriter and a better person. My big dreams inspire me to break the chains of fear and push me to believe that one day I will be the great man God intends for me to be." What do your big dreams inspire you to do?

There is a story of a father that had taken his children to the circus. As they were watching the big elephants perform, the father became intrigued by the fact that the huge creatures were being controlled by only a small rope tied to their front leg. There were no metal cages or large chains being used to hold the massive elephants from breaking out of the ring. It was obvious that the power of the elephants could allowed them, at any time, to break away from their bonds made of very tiny lines of rope. The tiny ropes were so small that they were barely visible from the seats in the arena, but the elephants never went beyond the limits of the rope. After the show was over, the father was able to get the attention of one of the trainers nearby and asked, "Why do the elephants never try to break the rope and attempt to get away?" "Well," the trainer said, "when circus elephants are very young and much smaller, we use the tiny ropes to tie them up. At that young age, it's enough to hold them. As they grow up, they are conditioned because of their amazing memories to believe they cannot break the rope. They remember that the rope held them back when they were small, and therefore, believe the rope still has the strength to hold them back as adults, even though they are now much bigger and stronger. So they never try to break free. Their memory, as elephants never forget, is used against them."

The man and his children thought that was the most amazing story. Animals weighing tons had the power and strength to break free from their captivity, but because they once did not have the power or strength, they believed they could never develop the power and strength. The elephants were held captive by their own past fears, frustrations, and failures.

Elephants do not have hopes and dreams. They have only memory and instinct. Like circus elephants, many of us go through life allowing the memories of some past unfavorable incident to hold us from believing our life can get better. We harbor the belief that there is nothing we can do to impact our lives, simply because we failed at something once before, or because we are fearful of failing. For too many of us, fear, frustration, and failure are the small ropes that hold us back. That is why it is so important that we do not consult our fears, frustrations, or failures. They keep us from dreaming big. They keep us from breaking the ropes that hold us back. Imagine if Maurice allowed his past failures to hold him back. Would he be featured in this book? Would he still be writing music? Would he still be on his path to greatness? If we do not allow ourselves to dream, then we never consider what is still possible for us to do. The elephant does not dream of having the strength to break the rope; therefore, it never considers breaking the rope is possible. The elephant is held back because when it was small, it failed at breaking the rope. So the elephant simply stops trying. When you stop dreaming, you stop trying. Failure is an integral and critical part of discovering who you are and what you are capable of; we should never give up on ourselves. If you fail, so what! Simply dream of succeeding the next time you try. If you fail again, try again. Be inspired by your dreams. If you dream big enough, you will eventually develop the inspiration, the power, and the strength to break the chains of your fears, frustrations, and failures. Do not allow the unpleasant memories of your past to be the reason you do not succeed tomorrow. Dream big! Be inspired! Break the ropes! Break the chains! Live an AMAZINGLY RIDICULOUS life!

6TH HABIT

NOW

Get in the NOW! Get TAPPED IN! Don't tell your Amazingly Ridiculous life to wait.

"Change will not come if we wait for some other person or some other time. We are the ones we've been waiting for. We are the change that we seek."

—Barack Obama, 44th President of the United States

Being in the NOW means you have an "I Never Quit", "I Own It", and "I Put in the Work" attitude. DO NOT Quit! Own It! Put in Work! You are the change that you seek! There is no one to wait for. Superman is not coming. There is not a better time coming. Get in the NOW! The quality of your life is determined by the quality of your actions. Far too often, current circumstances are offered for consideration as to why you made a bad decision or acted inappropriately. "I am a victim of circumstance" is an all-too-familiar reframe. Unfavorable social constructs and socio-economically disadvantaged conditions are not the reasons you will fail to rise in life. Also, living in conditions of social and economic advantage will not guarantee that you will rise in life. You must always possess the capacity to make the correct decision, to take the appropriate actions, to always have a tremendous impact on the human environment within which you intend to carve out your AMAZINGLY RIDICULOUS life.

Correct decisions and appropriate actions in life can be subjugated by four factors: Timing, Awareness, Position, and Preparation (TAPP). If you are in the right place, at the right time, aware of the opportunity, and prepared to take action; then you are "TAPPED IN!" If you are "TAPPED IN!", then any action you take will be appropriate and will produce a desired outcome. You will be able to take full advantage of situations when given the opportunity. If you are not in the right place, at the wrong time, unaware of the opportunity, and unprepared, then you are unable to act appropriately to take advantage of what life has presented to you; and you are "TAPPED OUT." At all moments in life, you are either "TAPPED IN!" or "TAPPED OUT"; which will ultimately determine the height, width, and depth of your travels. When "TAPPED OUT", you may not realize that you are the reason your circumstances are marred in undesirable and self-stultifying conditions. Your time is NOW! Commit to getting "TAPPED IN!" There is no time to waste waiting on someone else or some other time. You are the one you have been waiting for. When life presents an opportunity for an increase, you must be ready to act with assuredness and intrepidness. You must be vigilant, properly prepared, and ready to seize the opportunity at all times; and you must be ready to act with adequacy and without hesitation. Doubt and inadequacy causes you to be "TAPPED OUT." Doubt causes you to have no confidence in your timing and position. So you are never properly prepared. Inadequacy is the result of not fully recognizing the opportunity. So being "TAPPED OUT" causes you to never achieve your best because you are never quite ready to seize the opportunities that come your way. You end up settling for "good enough" or mediocrity. Don't settle! You can always do better in life. This holds true under all conditions, irrespective of current circumstance. So even if you are living in unfavorable conditions today, tomorrow can provide you the opportunity to better your situation; but you must be in the right place, at the right time, aware of the opportunity, and prepared to take action. If you are, your actions will be appropriate, and the quality of your life will increase without limits. Never Quit! Own It! Put in the Work! Get in the NOW! Get TAPPED IN! And go get yours today! You truly are the change you seek. So, get ready and stay ready.

Understand that a crisis will always reveal character. Character is what you build when you are acting in daily circumstances where no one is watching. You build character by staying in motion, exercising, reading, meditating, praying, developing your critical thinking and acting with discipline in your day-to-day experiences. Character is what you build when you are doing the small everyday things that are the nearest to you and the least meaningful to others. We oftentimes imagine that the crisis, when it comes, is where we will prove that we are the chosen ones, but the crisis will only show what we are already made of. The crisis will reveal the degree to which you have excelled in doing the mundane and most menial commonplace things. The characteristics we display in our immediate circumstances are indications of the characteristics we will display when things get tough, or tougher. You cannot get ready for the storm while in the middle of the storm. You get ready for the storm in the days, months, years leading up to the catastrophic event, not after the event hits. The great life essential to being TAPPED IN is the characteristics you develop in your private relationship to the life God has engineered on your behalf. The time will come when you can no longer hide behind the excuses or blame others, when your life is on full display in public places. You will find yourself in extreme challenge if you are not prepared, if you are not ready, if you have not previously developed the characteristics required to be TAPPED IN. Prepare yourself for your unseen life so when that time comes you will be fully ready to occupy this new greatness with assuredness and high expectations.

In life, doubt and hesitation can cause you to lose your place in line. Each person is a Zeitgiest; we exist in time, at a particular moment to do something special. We are spiritual time travelers of sort. So our timing is everything. Your place in line is a function of time. Chaos theory explains, our lives have a sensitive dependence on our initial conditions. If we leave our house five minutes later than planned, that five minutes can result in us being 45 minutes late because we get caught in bad traffic. So what time we arrive at a pre-selected destination is dependent (sensitively) on what time we depart. Imagine if Maurice "The Truth" had waited to move to Atlanta a year later than when he actually did. He would have been farther back in the line. He, perhaps, would have missed the opportunity to participate in this book. Timing is everything! And once you get there, on time hopefully, you never know who is watching. So Awareness, Position, and Preparation are really critical. A good friend of mine and a young actor in Hollywood, Keith Powers, says it this way, "When I am on set filming a television show or a movie, I do the little things that others may not. I ensure I display proper manners at all times. At the end of the filming day, I always offer to help clean up the studio and put away the equipment. I know the smallest of things can help make someone else's job easier, and I treat every person on the set as if he or she is the executive producer. In reality, you just never know who is the executive producer or CEO of the company who created the show or wrote the screenplay." Even when an actor is out at dinner or just shopping in LA, timing and awareness is critical. In Hollywood, an actor has no idea who he or she may run into. Therefore, they have to be prepared at all times. This preparation, the character building, does not occur on set while filming, but occurs at the mall shopping or out for dinner. In Hollywood, in the music industry, in everyday life, the real auditions in life and career can take place at the mall, at a concert, just hanging out at dinner with friends, on a college campus, or anywhere. That's really how sensitive life is to our initial timing, awareness, positioning, and preparation. Our lives, not just actors or hip hop artists, but all lives, benefit tremendously when we are "TAPPED IN." Maurice says that a secret to his success is he treats every person as if each person he encounters is the person who gets to decide, yes or no, to whether he will be successful in life. WOW! Now, just imagine if everyone approached life in a similar manner. Maurice also says, "When you're in the entertainment industry or the church ministry, you have to be professional at all times. When you step out of your house, staunch professionalism and Christ-like characteristics are demanded. In this new century, the camera is always rolling. Everyone is an actor, whether they want to be or not." That's being TAPPED IN!

We have to live in the NOW at every moment in our lives, if we want to live an AMAZINGLY RIDICULOUS life. We have to understand that we can't dwell on the past. Being in the NOW is about being ready and staying ready for the unseen. The camera is always rolling in life. Someone is always watching. It may be a music producer or Hollywood executive. It may be your boss at work, your children at home, or your spouse. Whoever may be looking, no matter what is going on in the real world around us, we have to be "TAPPED INTO THE NOW."

The next time you go to dinner, as you take your seat look around and notice others in the restaurant. Imagine the whole place is crawling with men and women who have the immediate power to decide the heights of your travels. Imagine there are others in the restaurant with the power to make your dreams come true. You must be prepared to present yourself as being fit and capable if opportunity presents itself, and you never know when the opportunity will arise. Get ready and stay ready! Does your chosen career require you to live in the NOW moment? Could you benefit from always being in the NOW? What if every time you left your house you knew you would run into someone that had the power to make a decision concerning a future job promotion, college application, sports scholarship, or acceptance into a social club on your behalf? Would that make you think about your school grades or work attendance differently? Would that also make you want to be at your best at all times? What if you were told that the next person you meet, at the mall or club or concert you were going to, would one day be your wife or husband, or your business partner or boss, or present you with a life-changing amazing opportunity? Would that have an impact on how you dressed or behaved in public? Would it encourage you to go to the gym and keep your body in good shape? Would it encourage you to be "TAPPED IN" at all times? Act as if you really don't have an option. Being in the NOW and being "TAPPED IN" are paramount to your success, but you have a choice. Choose to be "TAPPED IN" at all times and in the NOW. You just never know what the next moment will bring in your life. Get ready and stay ready, so that you are always ready. Whether you work in the music industry, Hollywood or at the mall; whether you are a fashion model or a college student; whether you are a professional athlete or a plumber, always live as if the camera is on. Live in the NOW and get TAPPED IN!

7TH HABIT

Gifted

Look within yourself and discover what God has already given you. You already have every gift you need to live an amazing life.

"What lies behind us and what lies before us are tiny matters compared to what lies within us."

– Ralph Waldo Emerson

There was once a gymnast who, in spite of her great physical ability and natural talent, never won a competition. She would always fall short when she needed a great score from the judges. She trained with coach after coach, trying to find someone who could make her a world champion, but no one could help the young gymnast win. Although she had the finest of skill and the best of training, she lacked confidence and focus. One day her parents sent her to speak with a psychotherapist concerning her lack of confidence and focus. The therapist agreed to help and said, "You must go into the darkness and find what is permanent within you." The gymnast was instructed to go home and create a space in which no light was present. Even the slightest glimmer of light had to be eliminated. She tried and tried, but just couldn't seem to eliminate all sources of light. Finally, she went into her bedroom closet and closed the door. She placed heavy blankets around the inside of the door frame and covered the entire door with more heavy blankets until all light had been eliminated. And just as the therapist had directed, she sat in the dark space with her eyes and mind open. After a few hours of no life-altering experience, she remembered what the therapist had said, "You must go into the darkness and find what is permanent within you." Suddenly she realized that by eliminating all sources of light that she was sitting in what was permanent—the darkness. Darkness has no source, therefore it is permanent. Anything with a source is temporary she discovered. All light has a source, sunlight, moonlight, fluorescent light; therefore, all light is temporary. When all sources of light are eliminated, the permanence of darkness is revealed. When you remove all sources of anything, all that is left is what is permanent. All heat has a source; therefore, all heat is temporary. The cold is what is permanent. The things behind us and before us have sources, thus temporary. That which is permanent is what lies within us.

The young gymnast then realized that her lack

of confidence and lack of focus had to have a source. She believed that if she could somehow eliminate the sources of her self-doubt and all of the sources of her distractions, then she could reveal what was really permanent within her and start to win competitions. Sitting in the darkness of her closet, she identified the sources of her self-doubt and mental distractions. She eliminated them one by one, and then she could clearly see what was permanent inside her—her gift of gymnastic ability and strong competitive nature. Her self-doubt and distractions were infringing upon her skills during competition. She had been more focused on the embarrassment of a fall or the disappointment of letting her family down. The permanent darkness became a vastness in which she swept all of her doubt and distractions into. All that was left was the gift that God had put inside her long before. The young gymnast went out and won every competition. She never lost again.

Our gifts are permanent. They have no source. They cannot be eliminated. They may go unused, but they can never be discarded. They can be squandered, and we can lose the ability to use them. For each of us, it is only the knowledge of our true gifts and our usage of our gifts that determine the quality of our lives and the profound nature in which we live for the benefit of ourselves and others. We can either use our gifts every day or we can squander them away. We can use our energy to become champions or we can waste our energy with distractions. We can confidently deploy our gifts in skillful manners or we can live our lives in doubt. We can go deep inside to that dark place in our soul, where there is no source of light, and grab hold of our true gifts and go have a grand old time being champions of life. Let there be no other option. Those that learn to find the permanent gifts God has placed inside each of us and focus on those gifts with confidence and concentration—instead of chasing the tiny matters that lie behind us and before us—will accumulate enormous character and achieve greatly each day, experiencing AMAZINGLY RIDICULOUS success in life. You will never lose again.

Maurice, just like the young gymnast in the story above, had to realize that his true gifts were already inside himself. He had to learn that anything he gained in Atlanta was temporary. He realized that the music that was stolen from him did not deprive him of the permanent gifts that were inside him. Maurice has learned that anything the entertainment industry gave him was temporary. Everything external to your soul has a source, and therefore, it is temporary. Maurice learned to find his dark closet where he could go and not let the industry, family, friends, or acquaintances—not even his enemies—taint who he is permanently. Character goes a long way. The previous chapter, *NOW*, I discusses how character is developed. Character is what's permanent inside us. Character also has the ability to take you to some amazing places and open some doors along the way. What we are permanently by nature has the ability to open all doors and produce our every win if we can avoid allowing self-doubt and despair to have the last word. Maurice says, "I have learned that life is not about learned and practiced talent most of the time, it's about who you really are by nature—permanently gifted. You have to be completely satisfied with who you are and have confidence in your own gifts." Mark Twain said, *"If everybody was satisfied with himself there would no need for heroes."* Imagine a world in which there are no heroes—everyone satisfied with themselves.

If you ever meet Maurice "The Truth" Willis, you will encounter a young man who has no heroes. Yes, he has in his life those who he looks up to with respect, and he understands that many people have helped him along the way; inspired him to use his gifts in a mighty way. But Maurice is extremely confident and completely satisfied with himself. He said, "I want to always remember how my grandmothers raised me. If I ever catch myself acting like I don't know who I am, I just remember my grandmothers, Miss Lois Willis and Miss Virginia Smith, both telling me that I am special and to always remember where I came from." I personally know Maurice's grandmothers. Lois Willis was my mother's oldest sister, my aunt. Virginia Smith was a pillar in the community of East Bakewell, TN. Both of these women were giant figures in the lives of so many boys and girls in our small hometown. These two great women are the very reasons Maurice is gifted permanently with good manners, a kind heart, and with respect for others. Those are the character traits his grandmothers embedded inside of him. When all of the industry-driven temporary values are removed, when he is home with his wife and children, Maurice is still the grandson of his grandmothers, Virginia and Lois.

One of Maurice's true gifts is he always tries to

make other people around him better. He goes to great length to see the best in everyone and to do the best that he knows how. Maurice has gone into his dark closet to realize that he couldn't go against who he was as a person just to be a star in the music industry. He knew that the temporary sources of things that tempted him when he first moved to Atlanta would not serve him well in the long run. In fact, those false senses of security caused him even greater insecurity, self-doubt and personal distractions. Maurice had to realize what his true gifts were and cherish those things enough to cultivate them and show them to the world; to be completely satisfied with who he is. By going into your dark closet and eliminating the sources that are preventing you from discovering your true gifts, you can truly focus with great confidence on just being the best you possible and having a wonderful life. Eliminate the temporary stuff and get to your permanent gifts. What you need to live an AMAZINGLY RIDICULOUS life is already gifted inside you. Live with confidence and win each time. Live without heroes. Be completely satisfied with yourself.

8TH HABIT

Love

Fall deeply, head-over-heels, in love with yourself. You must love yourself first before you can truly love anyone or anything else.

"You yourself, as much as anybody in the entire universe, deserve your love and affection"

— Buddha

Being successful comes with its ups and downs. Some people will love you and some will not. Great success has a tendency to make you a target. That's how I feel sometimes, especially when it seems so easy for some people on social media, mostly haters looking a hero and people not happy with themselves, to try to talk down on you, or bring you down, just for loving yourself. You have to love yourself in this life. I learned that I can't survive in the world without loving myself deeply. Life has a way of tearing us down and getting to the best of us at times. People can make you feel low about yourself and the path you are traveling. Getting turned down for jobs, not getting into the school of your choice, hearing negative gossip, and enduring bad childhood circumstances have a way of eating at your soul. Getting turned down a few times by book publishers made me start to believe that I was not good enough to be an author. Self-love and believing in my abilities became very important in those moments. Knowing I am good enough brings me great energy and allows me not to get down on myself. I have to remember that the industry is primarily controlled by a genre of people that only see green. Book publishing is a business, and I can't always take it personal. I want to write, and they want to make money. The two interests don't always align. I have learned that the people in the literary book industry will not always love you for who you are; they will only love you because you have the ability to help them make money. You set yourself up for disappointment if you rely on any industry to love you back. I have realized that the most import-ant love is self-love. I have to love myself first and love myself last, in this industry and in life. The reason my life AMAZINGLY RIDICULOUS is because I love me some me! I am an author and a publisher. Self-love drove me to free myself up from the opinions of others.

There are twelve habits of devotion in self-love: Appearance, Compassion, Creativity, Discernment, Forbearance, Forgiveness, Health, Knowledge, Meditation, Movement, Nutrition and Speech; Compassion being the greatest expression of self-love. Devotion to self is not simply a matter of being obedient to religious dogma. It is a matter of achieving the spiritual quality of God in yourself. This can be done only by self- discipline and self-cultivating the twelve habits of devotion in self-love.

Appearance: Your appearance—clothing, hair style, make-up, hygiene—says what you think about yourself. It is an expression of your state of mind. If you are conservative by nature, you tend to dress in a conservative manner. If you are flamboyant by nature, you tend to wear flashy and trendy clothing. Your appearance is the first thing people see and majorly influence their initial opinion of you. Make sure your appearance says about you exactly what you want it to say. Your appearance should say that you are deeply in love with yourself.

Compassion: Your compassion conveys to what degree your heart and spirit is open to others and things outside of you. This is why compassion is the greatest of the habits of devotion in self-love. Your devotion to yourself should be matched by your devotion to others. Your compassion is your obedience to God and a sure stand against evil. If your heart is pure with compassion, you will harbor no ill will toward any of God's creations. You will love yourself deeply and live in perfect harmony with the Universe. Your compassion is your ultimate expression of self-love.

Creativity: True self-love drives you to want to creatively contribute to society. Creativity is how we interact and contribute to mankind. Every person contributes based on their own creative ability. Some people may create music; others write poetry. Someone else may create smiles with comedy; while another may provide medicine to heal the sick. While some may create pottery out of clay; yet others contribute with performing art or perhaps visual art. However we contribute through creativity, we elevate our soul and the spirit of others around us. The more deeply you are in love with yourself, the more elevated the soul in its creativity.

Discernment: Discernment is your personal care and attendance to your overall well-being. We discern between right and wrong, wise and foolish behaviors, because we care about what happens. Self-love causes one to develop a deep interest in keeping out of harm's way. We become very selective, in a discerning and discriminatory manner, about whom our friends are and about whom we partner with when we love ourselves. You don't just step out with just anyone or whomever when you are deeply in love with yourself, you are very discriminatory with a keenly discerning nature. This habit must be carefully cultivated. The lack of discernment is why so many people make such poor decisions concerning who they let into their world. One bad apple really does spoil the whole bunch. If you really love yourself, you will choose your friends wisely. You will also discern painstakingly concerning who you fall in love with.

Forbearance: Your forbearance is the essential human essence of patience. You have heard that patience is a virtue, a good moral characteristic to possess. Well, patience is also an expression of self-love, a moral commitment to developing stalwart character, to always present yourself at your best. You have to be patient, not just with others, but with yourself as well. Forbearance is the patience to be true to who you are by nature. The power of your nature helps you overcome the constant ups and downs of life. Understand that fortune, good or bad, does not change who you are by nature. We must learn to love ourselves with such deep devotion that we are able to patiently weather both good times and bad, and all the while stay true to who we are. That's self-love! That's real love!

Forgiveness: Forgiveness is acknowledging God is love. Because of our spiritual connections with all humans we also know that we cannot cut those spiritual ties. Life is a contact sport. There is no true separation from others. Everyone is in the game. Artificial separations occur when, due to our egos, we are not able or willing to forgive. The secret to being able to forgive is always being able to see God. If you can truly see God you will also see Him in everyone you encounter. You will see him in everyone that hurts you. You will see God in everyone that disappoints you. But because you see God in yourself and everyone else, that also allows you to love and forgive yourself and others that have harmed your ego. Often times we must love ourselves to forgive ourselves before we can love others and forgive others. The spirit of forgiveness moves you beyond the artificial barrier of your ego and allows you to love yourself and others at all times. Always be willing to forgive; after all, you cannot separate yourself from the whole of mankind anyway. Forgiveness keeps self-love connected to the human spirit.

Health: Once we are giving life, everything we encounter is designed to cause our death. The balance between life and death is health. Our health determines the longevity and quality of our lives. If you love yourself deeply you will desire a long life that is lived well. Be healthy and thrive. Love yourself to good health! Visit the doctor annually for a health check-up. Learn to relax and eliminate stress. Remember, life is always trying to kill you. Learn how to naturally heal your body. Get a healthy dose of vitamin D from the sun on a daily basis. Take a hike in the mountains. Walk the sandy beaches. Swim in the ocean. Count the stars at night. Relax, love yourself, and live long.

Knowledge: Knowledge, not age makes a person wise. Get the best education possible. Gain intelligence to the degree you have capacity. Turn every moment of life into a classroom and value every learning opportunity. Whatever you learn, freely pass it on to others. Pay for knowledge, but give it away. It will come back to you multiplied. Intelligence is the one habit that you must cultivate every moment of every day. You can never have too much education, but you can be "mis-educated" by misinformation. If intelligence could be considered money, aspire to be a Gazillionaire! That's a lot of self-love.

Meditation: The mind does not rest until forced to. Meditation is forcing the mind to rest. The human mind goes from thought to thought to thought, without pausing in between thoughts. Your mind is working even in your sleep. Meditation is forcing the mind to pause between thoughts. That pause is rest, and rest is good for the mind. The longer the pause between thoughts, the longer you are allowing your mind to rest. Meditation is crucial to your health, intellect, and spiritual atonement. Meditate daily, if possible every morning before you start your daily routine. You can meditate with music, spiritual reading, chanting, images, and other activities as well. Mediation is loving yourself and taking care of your mind. Therefore, you should take care of yourself first each day before you give to others. Meditation detoxes the mind. It gives the mind rest. So it can be extremely beneficial to meditate a second time in the evening. Meditation allows you to conquer your unfavorable circumstances. It gives you clarity of thought and the victory over your distractions. Self-love is all about being victorious over the things that are holding you back.

Movement: Movement, exercise, keeps the energy in the body moving. Energy at rest is of no use. Energy must be moving to generate a force for action. The body must be in motion to generate the energy force for movement. You must exercise daily to keep the body moving, generating energy so you are always prepared to take physical action. Movement is vital to your health. Once you stop moving the body starts to decline. You cannot stop the aging process, but you can slow it down with movement. When the time comes for your life to come to an end, let it be because you have done everything you are here to do, not because you have stopped moving. Movement affects your appearance. Therefore, exercising the body three to four times a week gives the appearance that you are deeply in love with yourself.

Nutrition: Nutrition always affects your balance of health. Your diet should at all times be healthy, moderate, and disciplined. Eat living foods. If you want to live long, then you should have a diet that includes food that themselves support life. Green vegetation produces oxygen. Oxygen supports life; therefore, you should eat a diet that contains a healthy daily dose of plant-based fruits and vegetables. Not all foods are good for you. Ensure you eat to live, and live to love—love yourself.

Speech: Speech is reciting words, and it is also the practice of silence. Yes, you can speak without talking. Loving yourself deeply will allow you to learn when to speak and when to remain silent. Speech can be talking, chanting, singing, praying, reading, or reciting. Why is speech one of the twelve habits in the cultivation of self-love? Because your words become your reality. In the Bible's Book of Genesis, God created the heavens and the earth by speaking. God said, "Let there be…" With the same power, what we say becomes our reality. A few small words can start a war. Just as saying, "I forgive you" can prevent a war. "I'm sorry" are two of the most powerful words in the Universe. If "I'm sorry" is as powerful as the sun, then "I love you" has the power to move the earth enough to tilt it off its axis. Trying saying "I love you" to yourself. Did you feel the earth move??

If you are really interested in knowing how to create and sustain a deep love affair with yourself and have an AMAZINGLY RIDICULOUS life, just cultivate the twelve habits of devotion in self-love.

9TH HABIT

You

Be You! Believe in You. Be Content with You. Accept You.

"Because one believes in oneself, one doesn't try to convince others. Because one is content with oneself, one doesn't need others' approval. Because one accepts oneself, the whole world accepts him or her."

– Lao-Tzu

A man decides one day that he is totally unsatisfied with his life. He tells himself that he wants a completely different life. So he decides to just walk away from his life. After a long journey, he eventually comes to a gate, and the guard at the gate stops him and asked, "Where do you think you are going?" The man responded, "I don't like the life I have, so I am walking away from it." The guard responded, "You cannot pass through the gate and leave your life; the life you have is the life you have." The man asked, "Why not?" And the guard said, "Because you have a responsibility to be yourself." The guard added, "You cannot walk away from your life." So the man turned around and returned home. He sold everything he had and returned to the gate the next day to offer the guard a bribe of money. The guard stops him and asked, "What do you want?" The man asked the guard if he would take a bribe and allow him to pass through the gate. The guard said, "Yes, I will gladly take your bribe." The man handed the guard the money through the bars in the gate. The guard took the money and turned and walked away without opening the gate. The man yelled, "Hey! How are you going to take my money and just walk off?" The guard just kept walking away. The man turned around and returned home; except he had nothing to call his own. He had given all of his wealth to the guard. The man returned to the gate the next day, after borrowing money from all of his friends. He offered the guard the bribe of more money. The guard accepted the bribe, but again did not open the gate. The man returned to the gate every day with a new bribe; the man was committed to getting through the gate and walking away from the life he did not want anymore. He would borrow more money, steal money, and even attempt to disguise himself. The guard would always take the bribe and turn and walk away without opening the gate. Finally at the end of his life, the man returned to the gate one last time. This time he had no bribe, just a question. He asked the guard, "Can you just answer one question for this dying old man?" The guard said, "Sure." The man asked, "Has anyone ever gotten through the gate?" Without answering, the guard turned and walked away without looking back.

I have lived long enough to have experienced a variety of emotional circumstances—successes and failures, triumphs and fears, happiness and pain. I have now come to a crux in life where I question the purpose of my life. Why am I here? What does this all mean? Am I living the life I am meant to live? I have also reached the point in my life at which innocence has faded away. Self-awareness and self-determination has ushered into my mind a sense of doubt concerning my ability to have the life I want. I question, "Am I on the right path? Is my life positioned for maximum gain and success? Have I set the right goals?"

Love yourself enough to passionately want to be exactly who you are meant to be. If you do not, you will never accept the responsibility for being yourself. Others will not accept you either, and you will spend your entire life trying to walk away from your life. You cannot bribe the guard at the gate, no matter what you offer, because the guard at the gate is you. The guard at the gate is your past experiences—your successes, triumphs, and happiness—as well as your failures, fears, and frustrations. You cannot walk away from your life experiences or your perceptions. Those two aspects of your life go with you everywhere you go. That's why you cannot bribe the guard; you cannot bribe your own perceptions and experiences. Don't waste your entire life trying to walk away from your life; accept the responsibility for being you and commit to becoming the best you. Don't waste time bribing yourself or consulting the opinion of others. Don't live for the fake approval of others. Life comes with good days and with "not-so-good" days. No amount of money can change that fact. Just do you and love you, and your life will be just grand.

When talking with Maurice, he said one of the reasons his life is AMAZINGLY RIDICULOUS is because he accepts being Maurice Willis and all that life brings. He says, "I am not faking it. I am not trying to be anyone else. I am focused only on becoming the best I can be. Because I accept who I am, others accept me as well." Maurice has created his own brand. His dad was an alcoholic, and he accidentally killed himself while in a drunken stupor. His mother never made him and his siblings a priority in her life. Drugs were her focus. That's why Maurice was raised by his grandparents. He did what he needed to so he could take care of himself and his siblings, including hustling in the streets at one point. Maurice is the son of an alcoholic father and a mother addicted to drugs, but he is not running to the gate every day asking the guard to let him out of his life. He accepts being the son of an alcoholic and a drug user. Despite his upbringing, Maurice is making the absolute best of his life. Everyone is charged with doing the same. We have to make the best of this life; it's all that we have. We must hope, dream, hustle, and fight through life. The nature of a dreamer, hustler, and fighter is in all of us. Our dreamer nature allows us to walk into the auditions of life with vision and purpose, knock on doors and ask for our greatest hopes to materialize. Our hustle nature is why we are where we are right now. Our fight nature will be the reason we are where we are tomorrow. Maurice told me, "I dreamed, hustled, and fought to be where I am today. Where I am tomorrow will be because of my dreams, hustle, and fight today." Maurice has not walked up to the gate and tried to bribe the guard to get out of his life. "The Truth" in Maurice is his responsibility for being "True" to himself and others, and he accepts that responsibility.

So, whatever you are in this life, believe in yourself. Be content with yourself. Accept yourself. Don't apologize for being you and don't ask for permission. Don't run from who you are or who your parents may be or may not have been. No matter what failures, fears, or frustrations you or your family have faced, life has given you something that—if channeled into useful energy—will ensure your successes, triumphs, and happiness tomorrow. You can't walk away from your life, so why not make the best of it? After all, it is the only one you will ever have. As William Ernest Henley said in his poem, Invictus, "...*It matters not how strait the gate, How charged with punishment the scroll, I am the master of my fate; I am the captain of my soul.*" So, go make your life AMAZINGLY RIDICULOUS, irrespective of circumstance.

Life is a series of mountains and valleys that we travel in and out of, and up to and down from. There are no guarantees, and I don't believe God cares about our circumstances. He has power over our lives and gives us the power and the dominion to self-determine our fate and how we live, regardless of circumstance.

Invictus

Out of the night that covers me,
Black as the pit from pole to pole,
I thank whatever Gods may be,
For my unconquerable soul.

In the fell clutch of circumstance,
I have not winced nor cried aloud.
Under the bludgeoning of chance,
My head is bloody, but unbowed.

Beyond this place of wrath and tears
Looms but the Horror of the shade,
And yet the menace of the years
Finds and shall fine me unafraid.

It matters not how strait the gate,
How charged with punishments the scroll,
I am the master of my fate,
I am the captain of my soul.

—William Ernest Henley

In the above poem, *Invictus*, William Ernest Henley describes how a person should respond to life's challenges. The word "invictus" is Latin for "unconquerable" or "unbeatable." William Ernest Henley had tuberculosis of the bone in one leg. He wrote the poem, *Invictus*, during a stay in the hospital. The leg was eventually amputated when he was a fairly young man. William Ernest Henley was determined to not let the loss of one leg, or any of life's travails for that matter, get the best of him and conquer his soul or beat his spirit into submission. He went on to have a very successful life as a poet with just one leg.

It doesn't matter what unfavorable circumstances you are dealt in life, your life is your life. It's the only one you have. You have to be yourself. Everyone—whether you are an amputee, a poet, blind, a singer, deaf, an athlete, an actor, a cowgirl, a ballerina, a cancer patient, healthy, rich, or stricken with disease—has some challenge in life that you must overcome. You must be self-determined to not allow your life's challenges to conquer your soul or beat your spirit into the ground. Your soul really is unconquerable. Your spirit is unbeatable. You have to have the courage to accept the life you have been given and make the absolute best of it. Be AMAZINGLY RIDICULOUS! Be You!

Ridiculous

Be Ridiculous! It really is the very ingredient that makes life everything it can be.

"And where I excel is ridiculous, sickening, work ethic. You know, while the other guy's sleeping? I'm working."

—Will Smith

There is something better than utopia. It is the RIDICULOUS. Utopia is an imaginary impossibility. Being ridiculous is very possible. The ridiculousness of life is a spiritual zone where the impossible valiantly becomes the possible, where amazing things happen and you have no answer for how or why they happen. Ridiculous is Michael Jordan scoring at will against the defense and him shrugging his shoulders and throwing up his hands saying, "I don't know how every shot is going in. I'm just in this zone." That's what ridiculous is. It's knowing nothing or no one can stop you. You're ridiculous! You just are. Have you ever been doing something—driving a car, jamming to music, playing a sport or running a marathon—and you find yourself in a sweet spot, and you feel the enormous intensity of the moment? Ridiculous is also very intense. I can feel the intensity of the moment when I am traveling around the country speaking, the cameras are on, and I am executing my craft for the audience. I say to myself, "I don't want this moment to end." It gets that way when you are with your girl or your man, and you don't want the moment to end. It's intense; it's ridiculous; it's a zone.

Ridiculous people are amazing and phenomenal people. I believe they have something inside that others simply do not or they have figured something out that others haven't figured out yet. Or perhaps it's both. Ridiculous people have their own persona, it's not swag or gloating, it is something else; as if they know something that others do not, a secret of sort. The root word for ridiculous is ridicule. The definition of ridicule, according to the Merriam-Webster dictionary is, *"the act of making fun of someone or something in a cruel or harsh way: harsh comments made by people who are laughing at someone or something."* Everyone has been the subject of a joke or mockery of some sort. Each of us has been made fun of, ridiculed. The ridiculousness that I am referring to in this book is none of that. The ridiculous nature I am speaking of is redefined in the context of this literary work.

The meaning of ridiculous in the phrase "AMAZINGLY RIDICULOUS" is to have reached the highest possible realm in happiness, euphoria, accomplishment, passion, and natural ability, so that you are beyond some phenomenal or amazing state of being. You don't want it to end. You are RIDICULOUS!

The truth is, ridiculous people may very well not be ridiculous at all; they just seem to be that way because most other people haven't reached that highest realm in happiness, accomplishments, passion, or natural ability. Being ridiculous means you do not follow a common process to success; you don't adhere to rules or restrictions that hold others back. Being ridiculous means doing 10 times, 100 times, or 1,000 times more than the next person, if that is what it takes; because being ridiculous is intense. Being ridiculous is also a conscious choice. You have to choose to be ridiculous. There is nothing natural or automatic about being beyond amazing or about being above phenomenal. You have to want to be Michael Jordan taking the winning shot at the buzzer. Most people are just too serious to be ridiculous. Serious people are afraid of being ridiculed. Serious people are afraid of failure. They fear being laughed at so they never break the rules; they never take the winning shot. They always do what is expected. They prefer common place over unbridled accomplishment. Serious people prefer mediocrity over amazing. To get to the place where life is amazing, you have to be willing to take the ridiculous route. You have to want to take the winning shot.

Ridiculous people, like Will Smith stated in his cited quote, engage in the things others do not. They stay late and arrive early. They study longer and re-search more. They dream bigger and dare greater. Yes, ridiculous people are ridiculous because they dance to the beat of their own drums. Ridiculous people appear abnormal because everyone else is trying to be nor-mal and trying to fit in. Ridiculous people don't worry about fitting in; they enjoy being different; they work to get into the zone where the ridiculous happens. If you are different, be brave enough to remain different and be thankful that God has made you different; for being different means you are here to be AMAZINGLY RIDICULOUS.

In the story of David and Goliath, by every nat-ural measure David was supposed to lose his battle against Goliath. David was victorious because he was different and he embraced his difference. In fact, his difference gave him the advantage. Most other fighters would have fought Goliath in close combat and would have had to deal with Goliath's over-powering physi-cal strength. David did the opposite. David was small in physical stature, and he was a deadeye shot with his slingshot. David was also a shepherd who had no expe-rience in hand-to-hand combat. So he fought Goliath from a distance, just as he would ward off wolves from a distance when they would come to eat his sheep. As the story has it, David was known to have killed a bear with his slingshot. He was ridiculous; he could get into his zone. Goliath could not see very well because his eyes had been damaged in other fights. So when David slung that rock from his slingshot at a speed of roughly 100 mph, Goliath never saw the rock coming. So he could not duck or avoid the projectile. You know how the story ends. It is intense! David was willing to take the winning shot when no one else was willing to do so. David is written into history as being AMAZINGLY RIDICULOUS because he did the amazing in such an uncommonly ridiculous manner. He did the amazing by defeating Goliath. He did it in a ridiculous manner because he was different and was brave enough to remain different. I admire and respect those who are brave enough to remain different and go on, despite the odds against them and consciously decide to do the ridiculous. Remember, what makes you different very well could be what gives you the advantage.

There are so many people who consciously decided to be ridiculous, to be different. Below are just a few Ridiculous Americans that I admire and respect, not necessarily because of what they accomplished, but because of the manner in which they had to go about their business.

Dr. Dre – He is just a ridiculous Brother all around. He is the founder and CEO of Aftermath Entertainment and created Beats Electronics. He has produced some of the biggest names in rap and hip-hop. Dr. Dre became well known when he was in the group NWA, signed with Ruthless Records. He has starred in several Hollywood movies, and the movie "Straight Outta Compton" chronicled his time with the group NWA. He rose from the streets of Compton, CA to become the third richest figure in hip-hop today. That's ridiculous!

President Barrack Obama – The 44th President of the United States of America, a man of Black-African descent. Now, that's just ridiculous, and then some!!

Frederick Douglass – Quite possibly the most ridiculous of all, Frederick Douglass was a slave turned statesman. He put the entire race of African-Americans on his shoulders and stood alone in his staunch convictions. He fought for the rights of Black people well before there was even a notion of a civil rights movement. He is America's greatest champion of individual liberty. Oftentimes, Frederick would be beaten so badly that he could barely walk; but he would always make it to his next speaking engagement to deliver his fire and fury. He was not part of a moment of many people. He alone was the movement. That's ridiculous!

Patrick Willis – Patrick is one of my favorite professional athletes of all time. He played seven years in the NFL with the San Francisco 49ers. He made the All-Pro team each of the seven years. That is a rare feat to accomplish in the NFL. His workout, natural athletic ability, and his unrelenting desire to be a better player year after year were ridiculous. He rose from meager beginnings in Bruceton, TN to become one of the greatest linebackers of all time. His approach to the game and his commitment to be better year after year was ridiculous!

Will Smith – Will is an actor, producer, rapper, comedian, and songwriter. In 2007, Newsweek Magazine called him "the most powerful actor in Hollywood." As of 2016, his films have grossed $7.5 billion at the global box office. For a Brother from the west side of Philly, that's ridiculous!

Oprah Winfrey – Dubbed the "Queen of all Media", from rural Mississippi and born to a single teenage mother, Oprah is one of the most phenomenal humans to have ever lived. Her philanthropy alone is ridiculous! Owning her own television network is ridiculous! Being an African-American woman and being ranked as one of the most influential people in the world is ridiculous! Taking the Oprah Winfrey Show to the top-rated show of its kind in history to becoming an actress, producer, and philanthropist to becoming a billionaire; I don't know about you, but to me that is AMAZINGLY RIDICULOUS!

Michael Jackson, Ray Charles, Bill Gates, Steve Jobs, Stevie Wonder, Jamie Foxx, LeBron James, Kobe Bryant, Stephen Curry, Tom Brady, Bill Russell, Prince, Magic, Samuel L. Jackson, Larry Bird, Muhammad Ali, and Michael Jordan—just to name a few more—are all ridiculous!

There are many more that I could name, but what makes these Americans ridiculous? AMAZINGLY RIDICULOUS people do all of the following:
- Take uncommon actions in an uncommon manner
- Work harder than everyone else around them
- Deploy a radical imagination to accomplish radical achievements
- Create their own paths to follow and avoid the roads most traveled
- Mine the gold that is deep in their own soul and do not ask for permission
- Operate at a very high spiritual frequency and do not keep track of time
- Take advantage of every opportunity, and create opportunity if there is none
- Follow their passion without fear of failure; for failure is not an option

- Take the winning shot
- Love themselves enough to never give up on their dreams
- Stay up late and wake up early to be successful
- Constantly challenge what they believe they know

In addition to the above, and perhaps more importantly, Ridiculous people do not worry; they simply exist. Do not worry in life; simply be who you are meant to be. Be AMAZINGLY RIDICULOUS! In the Bible, Matthew 6:25 reads, "...do not worry about your life, what you will eat or drink, or about your body, what you will wear. Is not life more than food, and the body more than clothes?" Ridiculous people do not focus on the material things that dominate the attention of most others. They don't worry about success; they are success. They don't worry about being happy; they are happy. They don't worry about life; they are life. That's what makes them ridiculous. The reason most ridiculous people follow the dogma of, "Do not worry; simply be who you are", is because they realize that life is full of false innuendos, misleading stories and meaningless pursuits. Ridiculous people realize that the only meaningful pursuits in life are the very things that are after their own hearts. They know that following their passion is the only thing that makes life worth living, as passion is driven by the heart's desire.

"It's not what you look at that matters, it's what you see."
—Henry David Thoreau

Lastly, Ridiculous people do not focus on what they are looking at; their focus is on how they see the world and how they see themselves in the world. My being ridiculous is staying connected to how I see myself and how I see my world. There's a lot to look at in the image-driven world. The marketing industry is a major part of our view of the world. We tend to lean toward market-driven values. What you eat and how you look is a major concern for everyone in the world, but both are heavily influenced by social images, as opposed to self-determined self-worth. I have learned that those who are the most successful in this life are those who understand who they are and are not concerned with what everyone is thinking. Their focus is not food, clothing, or automobiles. They are brave enough to be who they are. Will Smith is still working when others are sleeping. I am awake at 3:42 in the morning writing this book. When others are sleeping, Will Smith and I are up working. Kobe Bryant said his success was less about his innate talent and more about his 3-a-days and 4-a-days. Kobe worked hard to advance his on-court skills by working out 3 and 4 times a day. Kobe had a RIDICULOUS work habit. That's why he was the greatest closer in the history of the NBA. "The Truth" Willis is also RIDICULOUS! He says, "I am constantly sharpening my tools by constantly reading, studying my favorite artists, staying in the studio, writing songs, and searching to understand what it is that I can still be successful at." Maurice told me that he does not want to be an artist who is simply looking, but one who sees the industry and his rightful place in it. By conscious decision, he is ridiculously obsessed with seeing everything going on with the world and striving to stay connected to the human Diaspora. Maurice stated that, "I am adamant about missing nothing. I want to always be the first person who recognizes who I am. I never want to lose sight of myself and my world. I know I can get better. I want to always know what I can work on. I need to see that in myself before others see it. My ridiculous is I am constantly working to get better. That's the passion that I follow. That's the passion that my heart creates." Now, that's RIDICULOUS! That's Oprah Winfrey and Kobe Bryant type of ridiculousness! What is your ridiculousness?

Ask yourself:
●Am I taking uncommon actions in an uncommon manner?
●Am I deploying a radical imagination to accomplish radical achievements?
●Am I creating my own paths to follow and avoiding the roads most traveled?
●Am I mining the gold that is deep in my own soul and not asking for permission?
●Am I operating at a very high spiritual frequency and not keeping track of time?
●Am I taking advantage of every opportunity and creating opportunity if there is none?
●Am I following my passion without fear of failure?
●Am I willing to take the winning shot?

If you are doing any of these, you are ridiculous. If you are doing all of them, you are AMAZINGLY RIDICULOUS!

Imagination

Your imagination is your art. Become a great artist and let your life be the greatest masterpiece you paint upon the world.

"The world is but a canvas to our imagination"

—Henry David Thoreau

Creative imagination is the highest of all human faculties. That was the basis of the Romantics philosophy. Albert Einstein said, *"The true sign of intelligence is not knowledge, but imagination."* So, artists, poets, musicians, writers, actresses, actors, and entertainers—gifted with wonderful creative imaginations—are the true geniuses of the universe. Therefore, you should choose imagination in abundance and become masterful in applying your imagination upon the world as your canvas.

There are distinct differences between our imagination and our dreams. Our big dreams are human experiences that involve the deepest unconscious regions of our minds. Scary dreams wake us up frightened and afraid, oftentimes in cold sweats. The good dreams make us want to never wake up and leave us with a harboring desire to make the dreams come true. I think dreams are the way that the mind recharges and makes corrections to our ill feelings. In many instances, whatever the sort of dreams we have, our dreams do not become our realities. They remain objective to our natural life, altered realities. In contrast, imagination, while a natural human experiences as well, is the process the mind uses to cast mental images of our conscious thoughts. We dream with our eyes and mind closed. We imagine with our mind and eyes wide open. Once an image is projected, through continued imagination we consider the possibilities of our thoughts and mentally mold the images into an idea that is much more believable than a wild, objectionable dream from closed eyes. We can't control our subconscious dreams, but we are able to manipulate the conscious thoughts of our opened imagination. When our big dreams linger, they push themselves into one of the 1,000 regions of our mind. We are then able to participate with a level of control that can make our dreams become a reality by re-imagining what is possible. When the conscious cooperation of our imagination, our creativity, our opened eyes, and all five human senses are joined, our big dreams then become very possible.

The mind is the most powerful energy force we know. When the imagination of thoughts is sharpened and focused on a singular point, the point comes alive. Our mind is so powerful that we can bring into reality anything we imagine—anything! Yet most of us leave our greatest thoughts abandoned in the darkest regions of our mind. The mind is an enormous vastness of energy in which most regions remain uncharted our entire life. In large part, we waste the most powerful force we control. We tend to access just enough of our mental energy to just get by. We leave the rest, the greatest part, unexamined and unused. Socrates said, *"The unexamined life was not worth living."* I believe all of life is worth living, but I also believe that to gain the most out of life you have to explore every inch of your mind and leave not one part unexamined. Your imagination is the degree to which you have examined all that is possible in this world. What becomes possible becomes believable. What becomes believable becomes an image. What becomes an image becomes reality. So imagine so that you can become.

When we focus on our greatest thoughts and concentrate the powerful force of the mind on the creative images of our imagination, we realize that we actually do have the ability to self-determine the quality and quantity of our life. When the mind is concentrated, the senses come together in a supernatural consciousness. Suddenly, your thoughts become your touch. Smell influences taste. Sight is a condition of sound. And sound controls your thoughts. It becomes a closed thought loop of believable tacit knowledge that can bring your every thought into reality. Take a moment and think of all the things that started as a conscious thought in your mind that became a reality once you applied the concentrated powerful energy force of your imagination. You are exactly what you have imagined you would be. Henry David Thoreau once wrote, *"I learned, at least, by my own experiment: that if one advances confidently in the direction of his dreams, and endeavors to live the life which he has imagined, he will meet with a success unexpected in common hours."* If you want to be successful, then imagine what that success is. If you want to be anything, imagine it. Your powerful mind will make it your reality. Take a moment and imagine everything you have learned in life. Realize there was a time when you knew absolutely nothing. Now do you see just how powerful your imagination is?

Imagination has been everything in Maurice's life. While he was born to unwed parents who were chemically dependent on drugs and alcohol, he imagined a greater life for himself outside of the small town of East Bakewell, TN. Maurice has a story that is all too familiar. How many of us are born into unfavorable circumstances? Maurice had the courage to imagine a better life, and the power of his mind joined with the images of his imagination, and he became a songwriter of the highest order. He became a great father to his children because he imagined being a better parent to his children than his parents had been to him. There are no permanent assignments in this life. We are free to exercise our will up the universe and become whatever we decide. Irrespective of who we are today or the circumstances we currently live in, tomorrow can look completely different. Just consider the ridiculous people discussed briefly previously. They first imagined that they would be ridiculous. If you are willing to imagine a better life for yourself, you will surely become what you imagine yourself becoming. Maurice is imagining himself becoming a prolific book author and highly sought after motivational speaker. Guess what he is becoming? This book is the result of his imagination. Imagination is critical in our lives. Actors and professional athletes have to imagine being the superstars they eventually become. Our imagination creates the image, and our mind provides the force that gives us the ability to create a particular aspect of our lives. We should never lose our imagination and the ability to re-cast ourselves into different human images if we are going to continue to be successful in life. We never quite know what direction life will require us to move in. Maurice moved to Atlanta, and then his imagination told him to move back to Chattanooga. Life works the same way for each of us, irrespective of our chosen paths. Everyone has to have the ability to re-cast themselves into the images our current life demands. Success demands the concentration of our powerful energy force to become something that we were not yesterday or last year. Life is a series of re-casting and re-imagining ourselves. Imagination is the life form that gives us the ability to re-shape our lives into the vision of the dream. I am because I first imagined that I would be. You are because you first imagined you would be. There is no substitute or a greater source of power than our very own imagination when it comes to living an AMAZINGLY RIDICULOUS life.

The world really is the canvas to your imagination. Think of when you first imagined being in college, composing a song, dating a particular boy or girl, or writing a book. Think of what you are imagining now. Are you imagining being an Olympian or actress? Do you imagine being a doctor, a professional athlete, a race car driver, a jockey in the Kentucky Derby, a computer app designer, or something even more amazing? Whatever it is, you have the power to be exactly who you want to be. Your creative imagination is the highest of all human faculties, and your mind is the greatest energy force you know. So take your great imagination, and the world as your canvas, and create a masterpiece out of your life. Dream Big, imagine with clarity and live an AMAZINGLY RIDICULOUS life.

12TH HABIT

Discovery

Dig into the depths of your own soul. That is where you will discover the real gold. All of the surface stuff is worthless.

"You have to reach down into the deepest regions of your soul to find the most precious treasure. Once you discover the treasure that lies in the depths of your own soul, live your life mining the gold inside you. You have to bring value to this world from within. Everything that derives from a source outside of the human soul is worthless."

—Ronald T. Hickey, Author, 12 INSIGHTS

If you listen quietly, the soul says the subconscious contains all the answers. Many soul searchers have gone into the wilderness of their own minds and have encountered both good spirits and bad spirits. Because we live an existence of duality, good and bad, the possibility of great discovery involves the threat of misfortune as well. We should accept, emphatically, that our subconscious thoughts are representing the unknown aspects of our own minds, our hopes and our fears, our dreams and our failures, our possibilities, and our frustrations. Subconscious dreaming is a process of discovery, of gradually learning how we function as spiritual beings. Digging to the depths of your mind can answer some questions you have about this human experience and help locate the treasures hidden deep inside the human soul. Just like exploring the deep regions of the black forest, the process of self-discovery can be very intriguing. Successful self-discovery is rising to an extreme level of joy and happiness. Self-discovery is to locate buried treasures without being tempted to compare yourself to others. You may ask if self-discovery is necessary. If you really want to know who you really are, there is no greater method than digging into your own mind, scraping the bottom of your own soul. Simple contemplation of life does not go deep enough; and mental evaluations do not bring one face-to-face with the person staring back at you in the mirror. The depths of the soul are the only places where you can discover who you really are. Enter your own mind and drive a shaft into your own soul and discover the gold within.

Malcolm X said, *"The examined life is painful."* Perhaps that is why so many refuse to turn inward to discover who they are. I think most know there is treasure down deep, but they also realize there is pain. The human endeavor is painful at times; but that fact should not prevent you from going after the greatest treasure you will ever find in life. That treasure is you. The joy of the treasure has the ability to eradicate the pain. Remember the story of the elephants in the chapter on Inspiration? The circuit elephants are held in captivity because of memories of the past. Pain holds us back in the same manner. We avoid the pain of the past, as a result we do not move forward. We should not consult the failures, fears, frustrations, or pain of the past. We should consider all that is to be gained and go for the gold, at all costs.

Oftentimes we stand at the precipice of our soul, that existential vastness of the human experience, and question if we can bring order and a sense of knowing to our lives. We also question if there is a higher power that is truly in control. These are legitimate concerns of the spirit. Such questions represent the very crux from which we move deeper into the precipice or we retreat to some seemingly safer position. The precipice of the soul is the rabbit hole. In life, each of us has to decide if we will slide into the depths and darkness of the rabbit hole and become enlightened with self-discovery or play it safe and never step into the valley of the unknown. I believe the questions of life are so important that we cannot rely on surface findings, spiritual teachings, or academic knowledge; but instead we must be willing to explore the rabbit hole and discover who we really are. We are creation designed. God ensures that our human abilities are consistent with His divine calling on our lives. Once you discover who you are, you will instinctively understand what you have been called to do. A world-renowned opera singer is born with such a magnificent voice that her natural talents and abilities are revealed very early in life. The opera singer simply has to discover herself to understand her calling. What you are here to accomplish becomes so crystal clear once you are able to match your innate gifts with your true calling. That's what awaits those who are brave enough to jump into the rabbit hole. The rabbit hole should not be frightening. It contains all of the possibilities of this life, and that should excite you. Take a peek into the vastness. Yell out your name, not simply with your voice, but with your soul. If you push your voice deep enough, your soul will answer you back. The answer you will hear is your confirmation that it is safe to jump in. With that assurance, be brave and explore with encouragement. You now have a constant companion to walk with while you are on this journey.

"Be brave enough to live life creatively. The creative is the place where no one else has ever been. You have to leave the city of your comfort and go into the wilderness of your intuition. You can't get there by bus, only hard work and risk and by not quite knowing what you are doing. What you'll discover will be wonderful. What you'll discover will be yourself."

—Alan Alda

Your life should involve you constantly striving to better yourself, and maturity should bring about change in how you think and in what you believe. Who you are should only be a reference point in your life, never the mark of your final destination. Your life should be like a map of the globe, and your goal should be to travel every square inch of the globe. If you have not operated in such a manner, then you have possibly wasted some years of your life. But now that you have come to the precipice of who you are and now that you are looking into your subconscious nature, it's time to make some fresh decisions about who you want to be and what you want to do with your life. Self-discovery is the first step. If you are like most people, currently you are not who you want to be, and therefore you are not doing what you want to do with your life. This is the source of your unhappiness at home and at work. Your life is out of alignment with the Universe. Your innate desires, talents, ambitions, passions, and visions are in complete misalignment of one another. Jump into the vast darkness of your untraveled soul and discover who you are. This knowledge will give you that very important reference point in your life. The knowledge of self allows you to self-determine where you are in life so you can ask yourself if where you are is where you want to be. Most of us are not living the lives that we really and truly want. That means we are not the best father, mother, son, daughter, husband, wife, friend, colleague, employee, teammate, or person for any of the stations we currently occupy. Becoming a better you and living an AMAZINGLY RIDICULOUS life is about the alignment of your current life with who you want to be in the future. And you have to be able to draw a line and connect those two points of reference if the journey is to be successful. Without that connecting line, you waste years wandering in the wilderness of your illusions, your illusions of who and where you are. Discover who you are. Answer the following 10 questions:

- Who are you?
- What do you want to do with your life?
- Where are you?
- Are you where you want to be?
- What do you want to be doing in 5 years?
- What do you want to be doing in 10 years?
- What do you admire the most about yourself?
- What is your purpose?
- What is your vision?
- What is your passion?

The answers to the above questions are the very things that help keep my life going in the direction I want to go in. I know who I am and where I am. I know who I want to be and where I want to go. Knowing who I am—self-discovery—connects my soul to the man I want to be. Maurice and I were having a discussion on his life's journey and the values he place on self-awareness. Maurice relayed to me that it's common for him to get offers to do a variety of performances and to lead praise and worship at a number of different churches. He expressed that if the opportunities do not align with his values and who he really is, then he does not engage. He says, "If you are not careful, you can make decisions that do not support your purpose in life." He said, "Early in my life I would accept any opportunity just to get my name out there. I later learned that it was better for me and the industry to express who I truly was and to voice how I wanted to present myself to the public. Everyone has do's and don'ts, or at least everyone should. If you don't know where you are going, then every road you take will get you lost." Maurice ended the conversation by saying, "Traveling the depths of my soul gave me the courage to be who I am and to know where I was at all times. The music industry is not the place where you want to be lost. I don't accept just any offer these days. The opportunities I accept have to be consistent with who I am as a man of God and align with my beliefs and values in this world." Maurice has dug deep into his own precipice. So he knows his soul is filled with gold, and he has to protect his precious treasure and keep it untarnished. Maurice knows that even if his decisions do not always please others, others in the industry have to respect the fact that he respects himself and who he is. You can make the same decisions for yourself. Self-discovery is really the first step in loving yourself and living an AMAZINGLY RIDICULOUS life.

13TH HABIT

_____

Immediacy

_____

Live in the Immediacy of your life. Tomorrow is not a guarantee, and yesterday may hold no value or no truths today.

"Young people live exactly today...and they live in the immediacy of their world. And it's important for us, people from an older generation to realize that a lot of our values, a lot of our truths, are no longer truths, no longer valuable."

—Walter Mosley

Every person must self-determine his or her own truth and walk in it. Your truth is always found in the immediacy of your life. Yesterday can be used as a guide, and only God knows what will happen tomorrow. All we have is today to figure out what is real about this life and what is not. What was true yesterday may not be true today. What was true an hour ago may not hold true at this very moment.

When you look in the mirror, can you see your truth?

When you awaken from sleeping, are you the same person that fell asleep?

When you are dreaming, are you conscious of your breath?

When you are angry, do you express love and admiration?

When you bathe, can you remember how you became dirty?

When you close your eyes, do you wish you had another life?

When you hold your grandmother's hand, does her touch make you smile?

When you are happy, can you feel the pain or struggle of others?

When you are tired, do you rest your mind?

When you are sad, can you remember the last time you were happy?

When you exercise, is there a true purpose?

When you practice self-discipline, are you happy with the outcome?

When you consider what others before you have done, do you find intrinsic value in their accomplishments? Are your grandparents' truths your truth? Do you accept the values and disciplines of the older generation as gospel? We must understand the difference between vision-inspired truth and blind truth. Truth with a vision illuminates the path that leads to your AMAZINGLY RIDICULOUS life. Your truth will take you exactly where you want to go. Blind truth, something you have adopted from someone else, or from yesterday, has no value in your life. Blind truth, at its worst, can become an unhealthy addiction. Blind truth is suffering for some cause because someone convinced you to jump in the car. Soon you just become addicted to the car ride. Truth must be connected to your own vision for it to be of value to you. Vision is a right now—this very moment—type of proposition. Tomorrow brings a whole new set of circumstances along with it; therefore, truth and vision may need to take on a totally different meaning from day-to-day in your life. That's precisely why you must walk in the immediacy of your own truth, because it's your own life. Not your mother's or your father's. Not your sister's or your brother's. Not your friend's or your cousin's. Yours.

Some people starve themselves because someone else says they are overweight. Some are self-mutilated because someone else doesn't like what they see. Some slouch because someone else makes them feel too tall. We develop a complex about ourselves because someone else forced their truth upon our vision of who we are. Then we berate, hate, punish, and deny ourselves because we are not living in the immediacy of our own truth. Twenty years later, we come to our senses and realize everything others have said about us or convinced us to accept as truth has led us to 99 problems; and being too short, too tall, too big, too small, or too something else is not one of the problems.

My brother-in-law, Robert "Bobby" Matthews, has won about 15 Emmy Awards. I say about because I have lost count, and I believe he has as well. Bobby is an amazing producer of sports programs and understands camera angles and how to get the best shots that ultimately result in what the viewing audience sees. His 15 Emmy Awards prove that he is great at what he does. I remember asking Bobby why we don't see many tall actors in movies and on television. If you notice, men and women in Hollywood are essentially the same physical height on average. Bobby educated me on camera angles. He said it is much easier on the camera if everyone on the set is the same height. You need only one camera angle if you are dealing with one height. The average person would not know this. A good friend of mine and actor, Keith Powers, is 6'3" in height. That is tall for an actor. His height can cause an issue with camera angles when other actors are typically six inches shorter. An actor Keith's height almost guarantees the need for multiple camera angles. Imagine where Keith Powers would be, or not be, if he had allowed someone else's truth to convince him that he was too tall to be an actor. Thirty years ago, a 6'3" person would have been overly challenged to find work in front of the camera in Hollywood, but being too tall to be an actor is yesterday's truth. There are so many truths from yesterday that are meaningless to today's generation. In Hollywood, the interests of the viewing audience changes over time. Likewise, in the music industry, the interests of the listening audience changes over time. So, actors like Keith and artists like Drake have to live in the IMMEDIACY of the truth about their industry and ensure they have a vision that gives their truth meaning. In the entertainment industry, artists must have a truth and a vision that leads them to bring their Tiger Woods-inspired "A" game any time they are in front of the camera or mic. Each of us has our own viewing and listening audiences as well. Someone is always listening and watching. Someone is always willing to offer their opinions. Hollywood has to listen to the opinions of the public. The music industry has to listen as well. You do not. You do not have to take on the opinions of others. An opinion is not a vision, and it definitely is not a truth. Be willing to live in the immediacy of your own vision-inspired truth.

Truth with a vision causes you to make an extra effort, study longer, stay later, arrive earlier, and give it your best at all times if that is what it takes to get an edge up on life. Living in the immediacy of your truth with a vision is unyielding. The human spirit is naturally competitive. Everyone is a warrior by nature, in the sense that we instinctively compete and compare constantly. Whether you are an actor, actress, singer, doctor, mailman, nurse, police officer, gymnast, lawyer, athlete, businesswoman, gamer, pharmacist, dancer, or any other great profession, you compete and compare yourself to others every single day of your life. In all cases of human spiritual competitiveness, our truth is the weapon we use against our opponents; and as any warrior, we do not yield to those who oppose our truth. Hollywood is very competitive. Fans are constantly identifying who their best actors are. We are constantly communicating to each other what the best TV show is. In my household, it is shows like Power, Greenleaf, Queen Sugar, and Empire that dominate our viewing. In another household, the line-up is totally different. Because of this we force phenomenal talent in the industry to be compared. We watch as an overly-talented Black female actress compares herself to other Black female actresses all the time. When people are able to speak with truth, vision, and honesty in the entertainment industry, they essentially will say that much younger and more talented actors and actresses are competition that keeps them in the immediacy. Actors attend movie premieres, the Oscars, and other events and shake hands and smile; not knowing really what someone truly is thinking. The truth is that in the immediacy of an actor's, athlete's, attorney's, doctor's, poet's, bus driver's, pharmacist's, or others' vision for themselves, they are not willing to yield an inch to the younger and improved versions. The competitive warrior that is inside a person is the same "truth warrior" inside each of us, and we compete in the immediacy of our vocation, chosen profession, and even within our own spirit with ourselves. Competition is all day, every day! It's not just in Hollywood. It's everyone's immediate truth.

The competitive nature is in all of us, but how we compete matters. Having a truth with a vision eliminates competing in fear, anger, and selfishness. Your truth, in the immediacy of your vision, keeps you aware of who you are and concentrates your actions toward the shape of the vision. If your vision is living an AMAZINGLY RIDICULOUS life, then competition becomes fierce. Actresses do not necessarily have any ill will toward a younger version of themselves. The more mature actress simply has no intentions of yielding any part of their AMAZINGLY RIDICULOUS life. Who would? The older basketball player does not yield to the younger draft pick without a fight. The veteran police officer does not yield to the rookie officer. We are warriors, and the truth about who we are is our weapon. It is the warrior in us that drives us to be competitive. Our competitiveness is what makes us great. In essence, we compete daily to remain true to ourselves. That's why the younger generations reject the values and truths of their parents and grandparents. Each generation self-identifies and fights to be themselves. They strive to live in their own truths and push their own values. You must do the same, in the immediacy. Being in the immediacy is allowing nothing to hold you back and getting yours today. That's why Maurice stopped accepting any opportunity that came his way. Maurice fights to remain true to himself, today and every day. The "truth warrior" in him rises above anything petty or superfluous and drives him toward his most profound truth. What is your truth about yourself? What is your vision for your life? Refuse the opinions of others and become a warrior that fights for your vision-inspired truth to stand, irrespective of the viewing and listening audience. Maurice "The Truth" Willis is a truth warrior. He is unyielding. The truth warrior in you should be unyielding, and the immediacy of the unyielding will be the reason you are living an AMAZINGLY RIDICULOUS life.

14TH HABIT

Complete

Live a complete three-dimensional life. Become Cubic in the length, width, and height of your life; and accept who you are — completely.

"Don't rely on someone else for your happiness and self-worth. Only you can be responsible for that. If you can't love and respect yourself – no one else will be able to make that happen. Accept who you are – completely; the good and the bad – and make changes as YOU see fit – not because you think someone else wants you to be different."

— Stacey Charter

So much today, especially among the Millennial generation, I see an America where everyone strives constantly to measure up to others. This desire to fit in and be what others expect you to be drives everyone to want more, more of meaningless things. To want incessantly for anything, never satisfied, is to be incomplete in some dimension. Young people living at home with their parents are styling $500 Prada designer sunglasses, wearing $700 Natasha Zinko double denim jeans and driving $90,000 Porsche Cayennes. And they still want more. Our wants are uncontrollable addictions, not human needs. Our wants also have us focused on just one dimension of life—self-centeredness. A $700 pair of jeans is not about anyone else. That's about you and your silly desire to look good in someone else's eyes. Perhaps material things, in some weird way, sucker us into believing we are everything we want to be. Or maybe we buy expensive worthless things to make ourselves feel better because we are not satisfied with who we are. We have to learn to accept who we are, even without the Pradas or the Porsche.

From one end of life to the other, everyone strives to succeed at feeling whole or complete in some aspect of life. We strive to satisfy our want, by any means necessary. But we are never satisfied! Drunken euphoria may not be the objective; but for most the insatiable desires of the heart produce the loud and continuous chorus, "I want MORE, MORE, MORE!!" We may not quite know exactly what will make our life complete, but the very distinct feeling of incompleteness is undeniable; oftentimes oppressive, and never satiated. What makes us feel so incomplete and never satisfied? Do we perceive happiness to be of infinite measure, and therefore believe the purpose of life is to collect worthless material things? Or is the pleasure of luxury items the most addictive drug we know? Perhaps the real issue of incompleteness is we have no human concept for what the true measures of a complete life are. What exactly is it that makes a person whole?

Most of us strive one dimensionally, in one direction, chasing to satisfy our own selfish desires. We seldom think about others, and we are slow to consider a higher spiritual power. We fail miserably at life because a one dimensional life, thinking only about ourselves, is not a complete life. We never feel whole or satisfied with anything because life is designed to be lived three-dimensionally, if it is to be a complete life. Satisfaction in life comes only from living a three-dimensional complete life. The Pradas, Natasha Kinkos, and the Porsches do not make us feel complete. If they did, we would not have Millionaires and Billionaires who are miserable with their lives. Until we embrace the true measures of a complete life as being three-dimensional, our labor, irrespective of the passion associated with it, will always be a downward force. Our achievements will be without meaning, and nothing we ever accomplish will have a measure of true success associated with it—at least not any meaningful measure. Money alone has never succeeded at making a person happy.

Let's consider a biblical metaphor of the measures of a complete life. In the book of Revelations, Chapter 21, John describes a vision of the "New Jerusalem" descending from Heaven. In part, John describes the "New Jerusalem" as being 12,000 stadia (7,200,000 feet) in length, and said the measurements of the walls of the new city were equal in length, width, and height. The "New Jerusalem" was cubic; 7,200,000 feet in all three dimensions. This is not an attempt to offer a layman's interpretation of religious text, as I am not suggesting that anyone consider me a master of Theology. My own insight has led me to believe John was not describing a heavenly place we could see at the end of life, but rather what we are to become during our lifetime here on earth. I believe John was describing what each person is to become while alive. Each person, in our lifetime, is to become metaphorically a "New Jerusalem." The "New Jerusalem" was complete because it was cubic, equal in its three dimensions: length, width, and height.

Dr. Martin Luther King, Jr. also referenced John's vision in Revelations in a sermon in which he described the "Dimensions of Life" as: *Length* is the measure of your own personal achievements in life; *Width* is the measure of your "other-people centeredness," how much you give to the care and well-being of others and their achievements in life; and *Height* is the measure of your reach up to God. To be complete, cubic, the measure of our success should be the same measure of the success of others around us. If we achieve, then we should help others achieve in equal measure. Then the measure of our reach up to God should be the same measure of our success and the success of others. Then we are CUBIC. Most of us give in great measure to only one dimension of life, and the other two measures are either completely ignored or insignificantly engaged. We are addicted to desire and encapsulated in a one-dimension abyss. We care primarily for our own well-being. We do not worry about others. We would rather buy an expensive purse than donate the money to charity. We would much rather go on any luxury vacation than go on a religious mission. This is the very reason a billionaire can be living such a downward and miserable life. No amount of money makes a person complete, and the lack of money doesn't limit a person from being complete. A person may have a life of great length, as he or she may have significant financial means; but his or her spirit can be dead, and he or she does nothing for others. Because that person's life is one dimensional and not complete, his or her life is full of dreary things, and there is no happiness in life. A person can spend their whole life caring for others, but forsake himself or herself spiritually and humanly. This person is incomplete as well. And there are others who may believe in giving all their time to living spiritually and having great height of life, while doing nothing for anyone, not even themselves. In all such cases, life is not complete. We feel empty because we have measurable substance in only one dimension. The greatest among us may achieve measurable substance in two of the three dimensions, perhaps. The grand pursuit of life is completeness—to be as cubic as the "New Jerusalem"—equally measured 7,200,000 feet in length, width, and height. Each of us, if we truly desire completeness, has to tend to the needs of others in equal measure to our care for ourselves, and we are to reach up to God in equal measure to our human achievement as well. Such lengths, widths, and heights are the measures of a complete life, and the cure for our uncontrollable want. Let's strive so that everyone wears Prada!

People of all social and racial backgrounds and economic means will continue the grand pursuit of happiness, love, fulfillment, and big bank accounts. I believe those are healthy and admirable pursuits in life. I know everyone is simply trying to live a "better" life. No one wants to be last; everyone wants to feel fulfilled, and no one wants to be broke. We just want to succeed by some measure in life. We want more in America! And in America, more is better, bigger is the goal, winning is the only option and uncontrollable want is king. This is the American Way of Life! But it does not make us complete. It does not bring us happiness and fulfillment.

When a person has accomplished something he or she is proud of, he or she wants to be recognized in some way. That recognition becomes a little measure of success on some level. Whether the will to achieve and excel is of a natural sense or of a personal motivation, everyone tends to want more out of this life. Everyone is chasing something; and success, happiness, love, and emotional wealth are measured in a variety of ways as we travel down Gulliver's path. However success is measured, I believe the reason we attempt to measure our successes and our triumphs in life is because we are ultimately striving to live that complete life. Even though we may not be aware of the gravitational force exerted upon our minds by this three-dimensional human existence, we work to find happiness. I believe we can find happiness, joy, love, and fulfillment if we work to be equal in all three measures of life. I know personally that I feel so much greater about myself when I help others achieve. I know my life would not be whole if I spiritually did not have a personal relationship with God. As I experience personal achievements as an actor, my length in life, I believe an equal measure of achievement should be experienced by someone else because of something my achievements allow me to do on their behalf. My life has to be about the well-being of others for me to be happy. I really and truly want to live an AMAZINGLY RIDICULOUS life; but I really and truly want others to have the same quality of life. What would the world be like if you were the only happy person living the good life? My reach up to God, my golden rod of measurement, just as the Angel did in the book of Revelations, measures the height of my understanding of God's Will. It also measures my commitment to being spiritually obedient to God's expectations. This measurement is equal to my length and width. The equal measures of my length, width, and height are the collective reasons that my life is so AMAZINGLY RIDICULOUS. Become complete and reach your life's full potential. Become the "New Jerusalem." Become CUBIC. Become whole.

15TH HABIT

Ultra

Take life to the ultra-limits, then discover what is beyond. Be fearless. Don't play yourself small.

Our Greatest Fear

Our greatest fear is not that we are inadequate,
but that we are powerful beyond measure.
It is our light, not our darkness; that frightens us.
We ask ourselves; Who am I to be brilliant,
gorgeous, handsome, talented and fabulous?
Actually, who are you not to be?
You are a child of God.

Your playing small does not serve the world.
There is nothing enlightened about shrinking
so that other people won't feel insecure around you.
We were born to make manifest the glory of God within us.

It is not just in some; it is in everyone.
And, as we let our own light shine, we consciously give
other people permission to do the same.
As we are liberated from our fear,
our presence automatically liberates others.

—Marianne Williamson

Like most, you push yourself hard to reach the ultra-limits of your involvements. You tell yourself the sky is the limit, and you shoot for the stars. Despite the many efforts you may take to increase yourself and push your limits, you will always fall short from time to time—perhaps more often than not. Some days you take two steps forward and then fall back three steps the next day. That is life. It comes with its highs and lows. You eliminate one unwanted condition, only to find yourself totally consumed in other unfavorable circumstances. When you inventory your successes and your failures, you may label your life accordingly. In spite of setbacks, you must continue to improve yourself. It can be challenging to free yourself from the plethora of snares that may be holding you back; but with grit, boldness, and determination you will be victorious.

Your own mind and your self-imposed limitations are the very reasons you do not reach the upper chambers of existence. You can truly elect to live an AMAZINGLY RIDICULOUS life; you just have to stop being the source that causes your failures. As humans, each one of us has a degree of intellect, a portion of ambition, and a measure of will. Intelligence, ambition, and will are the sources of human desire. Each one of us has an insatiable desire to live well, do something amazing, or to be a part of something big. We want something out of life – you want to have an impact. You develop detailed plans and complex strategies for getting what your heart desires. Once you have the desire for something in your heart, not just in your mind, you commit your life to satisfying the craving. You refuse to rest until what you desire is in your possession. We really do shoot for the stars, and when we get there we want more. We want more because we realize there is more. The sky is the limit only until you reach the sky and discover there is something beyond the sky. When you are hungry, you want food. Once you eat and have satisfied your hunger, you move on to other wants. Life encourages, perhaps even tempts, you to always further your quest for more. Do not resist the desires of the heart. Do not play yourself small simply because someone is telling you that you should be satisfied with less than what you are fully capable of. Remember the message you just read on living a "complete" life. Become cubic, and reach for the ultra-limits of this life and do so boldly and without fear of failure. Bruce Lee said, "Don't fear failure. Not failure, but low aim, is the crime. In great attempts it is glorious even to fail."

You must be prepared to accept failure without becoming discouraged. You must also expect to become frustrated at times, but do not turn back. As Marianne Williamson suggests, and rightfully so, you are brilliant, gorgeous, handsome, talented, and fabulous. Be have to be patient with yourself and work to separate yourself from the need to chase outward desires; but be willing to risk fatal fatigue chasing the ultra-limits of the heart. And when you get there, make sure your light shines bright. The very brightness of your illumination will give others the right to do the same. Your life in the upper room should encourage others to reach their ultra-limits as well. When you reach your ultra-limits, something spectacular will happen. You are at the very edge of what you know. You are at the peak of your intellectual capacity. It is at this very point that you are able to connect with other knowledge, learn from greater intellectuals, and increase the power of your mind to understand things you previously never considered. When you travel to the ultra-limits you are able to go into regions of your mind you have not been able to reach previously and you take on a higher sense of awareness—a higher sense of who you are. When you finally discover what is beyond, your life starts anew. Maurice shared with me that was precisely his experience when he moved to Atlanta to kick start his career in music production. His life started anew, not because of a new city, but because everything he knew previously became less significant. Maurice went to the edge of what he knew. He reached the sky and discovered that the sky was not the limit. He learned that there was more to be had. Maurice said, "I had to connect with my essence in a manner in which I had not previously done. I really learned who I was. I learned how strong my faith was. I learned how far my optimism would take me. I learned just how important it was to have a strong resolve. I was innocent again, and my imagination came alive in Atlanta." Sometimes we have to move beyond our comfort zones to truly discover what we are capable of. Had Maurice not moved to Atlanta, he would not be the person he is today. Perhaps you are not the person you could be because you have not been willing to take yourself to the ultra-limits of what you know. We find it much easier to remain where we are than to step out and expand. We may know that we are working in a dead-end job, involved in unproductive relationships, engaging in habits that are detrimental to our health, or just too scared of change. Maurice would not have dared to go to his limits if he had decided to never move from East Bakewell, TN. In fact, there are many in our home town of East Bakewell that could have benefited majorly from what life has to offer if they were only willing to travel to their ultra-limits. My cousin, Don Allen Johnson, as I wrote in the preface, is the greatest athlete I have ever seen. To this day, I have not seen a better basketball player or baseball player. Don Allen, or Pockets as we call him because he walks around with his hands in his pockets all the time, never left East Bakewell. Now he is approaching 70 years old, and he is still walking around the old neighborhood with his hands in his pockets. This is not an attempt to talk down on a relative. There are very few humans that I have cherished more than I cherish Don Allen. But this is a moment to share with others that talent alone does not guarantee success. You must be willing to take your success out into the world, wherever that may be, and give life all you possibly can. What is the point of being great at something if no one but you knows you are great? Maurice, unlike our many other relatives, was brave enough to take his talent out in the world; relying only on his faith in God. Going to your limits requires you to walk in the depths of your spirituality. You may not be aware, but everything you will ever need in life is also inside you. Maurice became a new person once he left home. He went to his ultra-limits and connected with what was beyond. Life oftentimes requires us to move beyond what we have always known, beyond our comfort, face-to-face with our fears, to discover what we are really made of. If you are willing to move outside of your comfort and face the unknown, you come to connect more deeply with your faith, resolve, and optimism. You will also connect with your fears, frustrations, and failures; but we have already agreed that we will not consult with our fear, frustrations, and failures, but only with what we are capable of doing. With such a conviction, you will discover what you are truly made of, and I promise you, you will love the AMAZINGLY RIDICULOUS you. This means you may have to relocate to another town, end an unhealthy relationship, take greater responsibility for your own well-being, face the fears and failures of your past, or commit to self-devotion. Maurice did it, and you can as well. Even now, Maurice says, "I constantly tell myself, Reece, you do not know everything." That one simple mantra keeps Maurice moving to the ultra-limits, to the edge of what he believes he knows.

Most people live at the center of their universe—their faith, optimism, innocence, and resolve. The center is safe. The center is where we are the most comfortable. It is also the place where we play ourselves small. We must move beyond comfort and convenience and be willing to walk through the valley of uncertainty and insecurity to get to the outer-edge of our human experience. We cannot grow toward the light of our truth by playing it safe, staying in the middle. At the ultra-limits, there is a new beginning, as everything you were or knew previously becomes miniscule, comparatively. You hope greater, dream bigger, and envision more vividly at the edge of what you know. This is the moment that you are at the height of your faith, your resolve, and your optimism. Everything becomes possible. You step into a new innocence and your imagination begins to play. New images emerge, and you make a powerful connection with your inner self. But you have to decide which direction your life will go in. You can turn back or go deeper into the spiritual essence of your life, but you must show a devout devotion to God. If you do, you can become everything you have ever imagined becoming. Remember, you can choose what is right for you, but only God can choose what is best. Choosing what is good or right is always the enemy to best. When you commit to spiritual devotion at the ultra-limits of your understanding, the universe will give you everything you ask for with your actions. Everyone around you will be empowered and inspired by your purpose. You will be AMAZINGLY RIDICULOUS, and you will give others the permission to be AMAZINGLY RIDICULOUS as well.

Leap

Take Quantum Leaps when possible, and move with intensity at all times.

"Every morning in Africa, when a gazelle wakes up, it knows it must outrun the fastest lion; or it will be killed. Every morning in Africa, when a lion wakes up, it knows it must run faster than the slowest gazelle; or it will starve. It doesn't matter whether you're the lion or the gazelle; when the sun comes up, you'd better be running."

—Christopher McDougall

Life in the African Serengeti is an intense existence. Whether you are a lion or a gazelle, you have to run for your life, everyday! Imagine what we could accomplish if we awakened each day and moved with the intensity of a lion or a gazelle in the Serengeti. What more could life be if we took quantum leaps in personal achievements when possible and worked so intensely every waking moment of the day? What if we all had a ridiculous work ethic like Will Smith? Most people have no such reference. Natural feelings of strong intensity have been replaced with commercialized artificial stimulations. Instead of eating right, exercising on a regular basis, and getting plenty of rest to gain natural energy, we drink $7.00 cups of coffee from Starbucks multiple times a day or sugary, caffeinated energy drinks to keep us going on commercialized artificial energy. Instead of making time to sit and talk and build intimate relationships with other humans, we communicate artificially through text messages and social media. Instead of developing that natural swag that brings much attention in public, we vaporize and sip on some over-priced vodka or cognac just to look cool. When we want true romance, we read a novel. When we want real love, we get a pet. Where is the intensity in life these days? Love, romance, intimacy, swag, and energy are all artificial stimulations that we engage based upon their market-driven values. Do we know the reason coffee, social media, alcohol, vaporizing, books, and television have replaced things that humans have the ability to do naturally?

A quantum leap is a great, sudden, increase or change in something. The increase or change is not continuous. It is a one-time event that occurs in a quick instance, and then the event is over. If you were walking at a steady pace, then suddenly jumped up in

the air and took the longest step you possibly could—
the jump, compared to your normal steps—would be
a quantum leap. The sudden jump would give you a
one-time great increase in your steps. Quantum leaps
are natural occurrences that take place when we are
engaged in natural human activities. Artificial stimulation has a devastating effect on our natural abilities.
Our good health is ruined when we do not exercise,
diet properly, or get enough rest. Human relationships
suffer when we rely solely on social media for human
contact. Vaporizing and drinking alcohol does not make
you cool. Having a dynamic personality is what makes
you cool. Swag cannot be purchased at Walmart, or
Macy's, or Nordstrom. Smoking and drinking has the
opposite negative effect on your natural personality,
not to mention what it does to your teeth. Artificial
stimulation prevents you from making quantum leaps
in your life because they nullify your ability to use your
natural energies. Artificial market-driven products give
us a false sense of who we are. $500 designer Prada
sunglasses and $700 Natasha Kinko double-denim
jeans do nothing for our natural life. They only feed
our fake selves, and you cannot fake intensity. Nice
things can be a great way of rewarding your hard work,
but you have to do the hard work first. You have to
get beyond the artificial tokens in life and look into the
natural places where you can jump and take a quantum leap forward. Those quantum leaps are the movements that take you directly where life is AMAZINGLY
RIDICULOUS. These are not everyday occurrences, but
when they do present themselves, you must be prepared to act with assuredness and intensity.

"We must walk consciously only part way toward our goal, and then leap in the dark to our success."

—Henry David Thoreau

Have you taken a quantum leap? A quantum leap for me was making the smart decision to feature Maurice "The Truth" Willis in this book. I had considered featuring a young actor out of Hollywood; two NFL megastars, one a National Football League Hall of Famer and the other a future Hall of Famer; and a 6-time Olympian. All four of my celebrity options were absolutely excellent choices. Either had the market power to give this book a major push; so why feature Maurice? This book will provide Maurice the opportunity to take a quantum leap, and Maurice will move with much more intensely every day promoting the book. Your quantum leap must be combined with very intense movement after the leap is complete. Otherwise, all you will accomplish is one jump in the air. The celebrities referenced above would have produced a big jump in the air, but they would not have moved with intensity afterwards, not with this book in their hands. Maurice will run with the intensity of a lion or gazelle in the Serengeti. He will do much more than produce a one-time jump up and down in the air. The big difference between Maurice and a celebrity, as it relates to the decision on who to feature for this book, is the difference between a helicopter ride and a long international flight on-board a 747. A helicopter gets in the air quickly and only flies a short distance. The 747 needs a long runway and a much longer time to get in the air, but once at flying altitude, the 747 can take you around the world. I intend to make this book available to everyone around the world interested in living an AMAZINGLY RIDICULOUS life. So, Maurice and I are lifting off in this 747. We have made a quantum leap toward our flying altitude; but now we must move with intensity as if we are running in the Serengeti. Maurice has called to talk to me every single day since we decided to partner in this AMAZINGLY RIDICULOUS endeavor; yes, every day, sometimes multiple times in a day. That's what intensity looks like. That's what an AMAZINGLY RIDICULOUS life looks like. Does your life convey such intensity in anything that you are doing? There's nothing artificial about Maurice's intensity. It's all natural. His life is this book. This book is his life. His life is AMAZINGLY RIDICULOUS!

The 19 AMAZINGLY RIDICULOUS HABITS in this book are precisely the habits Maurice and I have closely followed and represent when we are at our best. Being your best requires everything in you. Being your best requires your intensity. Constantly pushing yourself increases your natural energy; it makes you naturally cool. The book is making Maurice naturally cool, hip, and dope! Always working hard to make life grand, cool, hip, and dope moves you beyond your inhibitions and helps you leap over your obstacles. That's being intense! What are the opportunities in your life that allow you to make a quantum leap? Is it changing your careers? Is it making an apology? Is it taking a summer school class in high school or college? It is telling someone no? Is it telling someone yes? Is it moving out of state? Is it making up with a friend you have not spoken with in years? Is it quitting your job and starting your own business? Whatever it is, take the jump and move with intensity. Move with intensity at all times in your life. Move with the intensity of a lion or gazelle, as if your life depends on it.

When your life starts to lose its intensity, the jaws of the lion are quickly approaching, or the gazelle is slowly getting away. How do you know when life is about to devour you or you are about to starve? Your life is in trouble when artificial stimulation has become more important than natural experiences. Your life is suspect when how you look has become more important than how you behave. Your life is on a downward spiral when wearing $700 jeans has become more important than helping the disadvantaged. Your life is moving toward despair when market-driven values have become more important than creative energy. Your life is meaningless when convenience has become more important than the struggle. Your life is on the edge when comfort has become more important than helping the homeless and the destitute. Your life is drab when sending text messages has become more important than visiting your grandmother. Your life is useless when luxury has become more important than giving to charity. When travel has become more important than taking care of home; when loud outbursts have become more important than self-discipline; when self-gratification has become more important than helping others; when the celebrity megastar has become more important than your family; when the television show has become more important than your education; when selfish-ambition has become more important than righteous pursuits; and when social media has become more important than self-respect, then your life is severely devastated.

When you see these things happening, the sun is coming up in your life. The level of your intensity and your ability to take quantum leaps will determine the outcome. Whether you are the lion or the gazelle, when the sun comes up, you better be running! If you are able to run fast enough and with intensity, you will live an AMAZINGLY RIDICULOUS life.

"All growth is a leap in the dark, a spontaneous unpre-meditated act without the benefit of experience."

—Henry Miller

17TH HABIT

Overachieve

Don't be mediocre. Overachieve in all that you do! Overachievement will drive you to nobility; to being impressive, courageous, generous, trustworthy, and at the highest state of self-awareness; all of which, you should want in abundance.

"There is nothing noble about being superior to some other man. The true nobility is in being superior to your previous self."

– Hindu Proverb

There is a level of achievement that says you are impressive, courageous, trustworthy, generous, and of the highest state of self-awareness. You cannot get to that level by being mediocre in life. It requires working not just to be above average, but to go over and well beyond, to overachieve. This is not an exercise of simply having an overabundance in your life, but rather becoming a noble subject in this human experiment. Nobility is an extremely rare attribute in human skin. Ask yourself who you may know that you would characterize as noble; impressive spiritually and intellectually, courageous enough to be exactly who they are, generous with their love and kindness, and trustworthy of your most precious emotions and virtues. Ask yourself who you may know that is of the highest state of self-awareness. Nobility is not a staunch condition of existing abundantly superior to another person. It is walking in the light of your own truth and being much better than you were yesterday. Overachievers are individuals who perform greater or achieve more excessively than they previously expected. The clear notion is the "overachiever" is achieving better results through intense efforts. In a practical context, "overachiever" is a social connotation applied to a person who does something, not just marginally, but significantly greater than some other person or persons. In essence, the term "overachiever" refers to a process in which the actions, intelligence, or spirit of an individual is compared to the actions, intelligence, or spirit of another person or persons of equal measure. The "overachiever" beats others by a significant margin of some measurement. For someone to overachieve, someone else has underachieved or achieved at average while performing the same or similar task. Or perhaps someone achieved beyond his or her typical performance. In either case, a comparison is made. In true nobility, the comparison is only to your previous self, not to others.

An "Overachiever" in accordance to the lastest edition of the Merriam-Webster dictionary is, *"One who achieves success over and above the standard or expected level, especially at an early age."* While the notion of overachievement is widely accepted by society, I believe it must be put into proper context for the notion of over- and underachievement to be of any use to us:

● "Standard" or "Expected" level implies that there is an arbitrary measure that a group of people are being tested against. The test itself guarantees that the application of a label (Standard, Below Standard, Above Standard or Meets Expectation, Does not Meet Expectation, Exceeds Expectation). Self-determination and innate abilities become compromised by a keenly established arbitrary standard or expectation.

● Overachievement and Underachievement are labels which implicitly affect our own behaviors based on a standard. Labels often times become self-fulfilling prophecies. As I wrote in my book, The Hoola Hoop Paradigm, *"We are always right about ourselves. If we say we can, we can. If we say we can't, we can't."*

● Levels of achievement are based on evolving, therefore incomplete, understanding of the true nature of human behavior. Human behavior cannot be separated from a person's complex issues or personal perceptions in any manner that is testable or equally weighted. Essentially, humans will always achieve differently when compared to each other. The only meaningful measure of achievement is the measure of what a person is capable of when he or she is at his or her best, not subjected to an arbitrary standard; nobility being the goal.

When we compare our achievements to the achievements of others, we drive ourselves toward either self-grandiosity or self-degradation. Both have the ability of causing the development of unhealthy psychological complexes. Comparing oneself to others puts one on the path of always feeling that no matter what one accomplishes, it will never be enough. Or one goes through life believing one has done enough because one always achieves above an arbitrary standard. Remember, good enough is the enemy of best. The only healthy comparison to make in life is against your self-determined ability. Once you establish an understanding of what you are capable of based on your personal assessment, work every day to better what you did the day before. Life is about reaching your zenith, coming to your peak, taking your leaps, using your imagination, creating an AMAZINGLY RIDICULOUS life—in abundance.

Is there is a fine line between being an overachiever and comparing yourself to your previous self? A person can find themselves chasing perfection, which does not exist in human skin. Many people drive themselves to unhealthy behaviors by pursuing perfection and establishing personal achievement goals, standards, and expectations that are unrealistically high and unattainable. You set yourself up for failure by setting unattainable standards and expectations. I understand that it is difficult to traverse life without looking to the left or right and comparing yourself to others. A quick look to see who's ahead can be damaging if it causes you to set unreasonable goals for yourself. Proceed through life with caution. There are extreme dangers associated with always looking around and comparing yourself with others. You want to make sure you set yourself up for success daily. Success increases your self-esteem. So give yourself goals that require you to reach beyond what you believe is capable, but realistic enough that allows you to be successful. If you faint at the sight of blood, it may not be a good idea to set a goal of becoming a doctor. If you know you were born with two left feet, ballet dancing as a career goal may not be the best thing for your self-esteem. Like many high school-aged kids, I played sports in high school. When I realized early in high school that professional sports would not be in my future, I didn't keep setting myself up for failure. I never dreamed of being a professional athlete, a movie star or any other celebrity. I did not establish unrealistic goals once I understood the obstacles in my way. I was not good enough for professional sports. I cannot sing. I cannot play any musical instrument. There are many talents that I do not have. I looked inside and asked myself what I believed I was capable of. I knew I was gifted intellectually. I was great at math and I love literature. I knew I had excellent writing ability and excelled at critical thinking. I did not have the physical stats for sports, but I had the intellectual stats for careers that required you to have a strong aptitude for mathematical computation, manipulating information, and designing process patterns to improve systemic operations. So I joined the United States Navy and became a Nuclear Engineer. That's what I had the stats for. In that capacity, I have always had a drive to overachieve—become a subject of nobility. When I am in my ridiculous zone, I am not trying to be better than someone else. I am trying to be the best analyzer, the best critical thinker, the best engineer, and the best writer I know I can be, based on my own standards and expectations. I work daily to become better than I was yesterday. This book is better written than all of my previous books. The next book I write will be better than this book. I compare myself only to whom and what I was yesterday. My goals and standards are high, and require me to stretch myself to my limits; but they are realistic and attainable. I set myself up for my success. I walk in the light of my truth. I believe I have reached true nobility, and because of that, I am living an AMAZINGLY RIDICULOUS life.

"We are always more anxious to be distinguished for a talent which we do not possess, than to be praised for the fifteen which we do posses."

—Mark Twain

Overachievement does not require you to run touchdowns, make tackles, shoot 3-point shots, run the mile under four minutes. Nobility does not require you to be a great singer, the leading man in a movie, or to create the next big thing. You don't need to wish for a talent you don't have. You simply need to approach the fifteen talents you do have with drive, determination, passion, and high energy. When I show up to work every day, whether I am writing a book, publishing a book, being the CEO of my companies, or being a Leadership Development Consultant, I show up to work with the drive, determination, passion, and energy of an overachiever. With an overachievement mindset, I approach my talents with a RIDICULOUS work ethic. I go over and beyond to ensure I am successful and to ensure those around me have every opportunity to be successful as well. I am always searching for the next endeavor that I believe will push me to increase my many talents. I have set goals that I know are aggressive, but attainable. Hickey Associates & Hickey will be one of the leading Leadership Development consulting firms one day, and Hickey House Books is destined be a major publishing house one day. I strive to be impressive, courageous, generous, trustworthy, and highly self-aware; I work to be noble. What are your realistic and attainable goals that will lead you to nobility?

To achieve true nobility:

●Establish your expectation for being impressive and exceed that expectation every day.

●Establish your standard for courage, generosity, and trustworthiness and exceed those standards every day.

●Set three overachieving, reasonable, and attainable goals that require you to stretch.

●Understand your level of spiritual self-awareness and exceed that level every day.

●Every day, identify one thing you will do better today than you did yesterday.

●At the end of each day, list your every success and set new goals for tomorrow.

●Recite daily: "Today, I will be impressive, courageous, generous, and trustworthy. I will be noble."

Overachievement, in the spirit of nobility, gives you a great sense that you are capable of reaching your goals when you give it your best. We are a complex web of emotions that drive us to achieve. Humans need to feel some sense of accomplishment and fulfillment. Without that feeling of success, we sink into a valley of despair. When we are kind to ourselves and patient with ourselves and give ourselves the opportunity to be successful, it is AMAZINGLY RIDICULOUS what we can accomplish. Don't look for shortcuts and quick fixes in life. Don't allow the endless pursuit of perfection to be your downfall. Overachievement is a healthy dose of self-love. Sprinkle some of it all over everything you do and watch what happens. Watch your self-esteem soar to the stars. Watch your list of successes grow. Watch how courageous, generous, and trustworthy you become. Watch how impressive and self-aware you become. An abundance of these things are absolutely necessary for you to have a sense of fulfillment and a life that is AMAZINGLY RIDICULOUS.

18TH HABIT

Universe

Force your will upon your world and make the universe bend in your favor.

"The Universe doesn't give you what you ask for with your thoughts; it gives you what you demand with your actions."

—Dr. Steve Maraboli

Make your stand today and force your will upon the world. Make today your new beginning. All of your hopes and dreams are possible when they contain the best of your actions, your optimism, your faith, and your passion. The first thing you must do is make the decision to commit to daily self-cultivation. You must make a strong connection to your inner-being. Outside matters are meaningless; you negotiate all of life's challenges with inner drive and your inner toughness. Therefore, you and you alone must make something of yourself, and in the process make the universe bend in your favor. The universe does not give you what you asked for when you sit idle and do nothing. It will give you what you demand with your actions. Once the arches of the universe curve in your direction, you will have the energy and power to transform yourself into the proper instruments for experiencing the deepest regions of your mind and spirit—the essence of your life.

Once you make your decision, all energy and power will come to you. Auspicious signs will appear as confirmation that you have the power to transform your world into whatever you envision it to be. With such power and a matched devotion, you can even make your fallen hopes and abandoned dreams come back alive. In the same manner, once you choose to commit to traveling the 1,000 regions of your mind, even the things you once considered to be impossible will rise to the notion of your purpose. At that very point, you will know the universe bends to your will, and your life will become everything you hope and dream. You simply need to take action on your own behalf, with strong will and dogged determination. The universe will give you what you demand with your vast actions. The universe truly is your friend.

You must know that life is worthwhile. You must realize that every action you take will produce an outcome. Act to produce outcomes that show your worth in the world. It doesn't matter what your life has been previously. Commit today with your actions to making your life everything it can be. Sometimes it takes a while before you see the benefits of your vast actions. You have to be patient with yourself. Don't try to find shortcuts. An AMAZINGLY RIDICULOUS life will require hard work, grit, determination, and doing the right things, not just sometimes, but all the time. Many people look at the life of Maurice, and others like him, and wonder what he has that others do not. Maurice, like many AMAZINGLY RIDICULOUS people, came from the bottom, and he is rising to the top. Maurice has no special access to the universe or the ear of God. The universe is set to reward anyone who is willing to act on their own behalf and to remain committed to the action they have chosen to commit to. Maurice has not gotten everything he has asked for, hoped for, or dreamed of. In fact, he is still waiting for some of his biggest dreams to come true. Remember, you have to be patient. Like Maurice, you cannot allow the denials of the universe to determine your path in life. In one conversation, Maurice said he made a commitment to living an AMAZINGLY RIDICULOUS life, and his commitment and the actions he has taken are the reasons he is where he is today. Maurice told me, "I did not ask the universe simply with my thoughts. I took actions. I relocated. I listened to my mentors. I studied. I read. I prayed. I kept a positive attitude. I gave my absolute best every opportunity the universe has provided. I eat properly. I take action." Ask yourself what you are able to commit to. Then take the necessary actions. The universe will give you what your actions are asking for. This book, AMAZINGLY RIDICULOUS is the result of my demands of the universe with my actions.

You do not need to covet what someone else has for you to be AMAZINGLY RIDICULOUS. You simply need to be yourself and tap into who you are and the gifts that you have been blessed with. God gives us all gifts and talents. Some may have only one gift, others may have five gifts, while others are blessed with ten. Don't count your gifts or talents for the sake of comparison. I spoke about the dangers of comparing yourself to others previously in the habit on Overachieve. Know how many gifts or talents you have so that you know when you have doubled your talents. No matter what we have been blessed with, God expects us to take the appropriate action to double what he has blessed us with. The Bible's book of Matthew, Chapter 25, starting at verse 14, tells us that when we double our talents we are given even greater blessings. That is precisely why you see people who seem to have it all. They keep taking the actions to double their talents, and God and the universe keeps blessing them with more. If you have one gift, double it to two. If you have five talents, double them to ten. If you have ten talents, you are to double them to twenty. If you look around, you can see evidence of those whom have doubled their gifts and talents; and as a result, you see that they have been blessed to receive even greater blessings. Hard work pays off!! In fact, that's all that pays off. But you have to be willing to put in the work. No one owes you anything in this life—not your parents, not your friends, and definitely not society. God is the "Pay-off Man." You put in the work and the universe will bend in your favor.

There was once a poor man who worked for a very rich business man. The poor man did odd jobs for the rich man, such as running errands, washing all vehicles, landscaping the grounds of the mansion, and fixing broken things around the home. The poor man was paid a small sum of money for his time and labor. The poor man wanted to be rich like the rich business man, so he decided he would save every dollar he was paid. He slept out back in the 12-car garage. He never went to dinner or had any fun. He would only eat what the cook in the main house would give him. He never went to the movies, a concert, or enjoyed any form of entertainment. He did not study, learn anything new, or go to a trade school to learn a skill that could possibly result in a better paying job. He never did anything to increase his talents or gifts. All he did was save the few dollars he was paid each week. He never bought any new clothes or the latest video games. In fact, he never left the property except to run errands for the rich man. He put all of his money in a large potato sack, and he would hoist the sack up by a rope each night so the sack of money hung high in the rafters above his head as he slept. He kept the money high in the rafters to keep it away from thieves, and he slept right under the sack so he could keep his eye on the money in the middle of the night. For years he lived in this manner; like a hermit hoarding money. He did nothing to better himself and just saved his money. After many years, the sack was full of money and extremely heavy as he would hoist it up into the rafters of the garage each night. One night while he was sleeping with the large heavy sack of money suspended above his head, a rat climbed onto the rafter and chewed through the rope that was holding the sack. The sack fell on top of the poor man's head and killed him instantly.

If you don't use what you have been blessed with and take strong actions toward making something out of your life, the gifts and talents, even when it is just one, will be taken from you; and your life will be taken from you. God and the universe expect you to live as if your life is worthwhile. There is an unspoken expectation that you must make something of yourself. This life is designed to harshly punish you if you do nothing and reward you greatly if you act with determination, destination, and delineation. Making money cannot be your only goal if you expect to have an AMAZINGLY RIDICULOUS life. Don't let getting rich cost you your life; that's too great of a price to pay just for money. As Henry David Thoreau once wrote, *"The price of anything is the amount of life you exchange for it."* Life is a strange proposition. The more we get, the more we want. The more successful we become, the greater we struggle. We have to learn to accept life for what it is without consulting our frustrations, fears, and failures. We must act with purpose, vision, and passion and make sure that what we are giving our lives to is worth the price we pay with our lives. The universe can be slow to respond. Sometimes what we are demanding with our actions may not show up until the end of the day, at the end of the week, or at the first of the month. There are even times that some things we are demanding will not come until the end of life. But trust me—it will come—and when it does, it will make your life all the worthwhile. An amazing life does not happen overnight, but it will happen. When it does finally show up, the joyous feeling of fulfillment will come with such a boisterous sound that it will make your soul stand still. When your soul becomes serene, that is your auspicious sign that the arch of the universe has turned in your favor and God is multiplying your blessings. Ask the universe with your actions and become AMAZINGLY RIDICULOUS.

Switch

Switch the Power on! Be Brilliant! Be Independent! Be Grand! Be BIG!!! Today your life really begins!

"The best day of your life is the one on which you decide your life is your own. No apologies or excuses. No one to lean on, rely on, or blame. The gift is yours – it is an amazing journey – and you alone are responsible for the quality of it. This is the day your life really begins."

– Bob Moawad

   People spend their entire lives searching outwardly for success, happiness, harmony, strength, and fulfillment. Those sacred attributes are within. They derive from the potential power of your brilliance, independence, and grandiosity, that which is already in you. You simply have to reach inside yourself and switch the power on. Such things are not found in a magazine, on social media, in the storyline of a movie or on television show. Your mind controls each of these functions. The average person accesses their central power sparingly throughout life. You have to learn how to connect with your central energy and switch on the power that's so magnificent that it makes you literally a supernatural being—metaphysically. First you have to understand that it is futile to search outside of yourself for anything of value. But if you were to inventory your most profound experiences, you will identify evidence of the existence of supernatural powers within you. We all have it—every one of us. You have the power to decide your life is your own. Offer no apologies and extend no excuses. Rely only on what is within you. It will be enough to transport you into the sacred places where you will find your success, your happiness, your harmony, your strength, and your fulfillment. Switch your Power on! Be Brilliant! Be Independent! Be Grand! Be BIG! Today your AMAZINGLY RIDICULOUS, life begins!

When you switch your power on, your innate energy channels must be clear for your brilliance, your independence, and your grandiosity to be of use to you. If your channels have blockage due to self-doubt, self-stultification, under-education, jealousy, fear, or slothfulness, then energy will not flow properly; and your blockages are a detriment to your well-being. Clogged energy channels are a "You" issue. There is no one else to blame when you have not found success, happiness, harmony, strength, or fulfillment. It's all on

You! All adversity is a creation of your mind, caused by the clogged energy channels preventing your powerful energy centers from having an impact on your life. Switch your power on and turn your energy up to the highest level. Then RIP OFF THE KNOB! Anything less is counter-productive to you becoming the absolute best you possible.

With your energy flowing—unrestricted, at its highest level—you are able to claim your life as your own. You are capable of being BIG—Brilliant, Independent, and Grand. Your brilliance gives you the confidence that you have everything it takes to be successful, happy, and fulfilled. Your independence gives you the wherewithal to live your life free from the opinions of others. Your grandiosity gives you the nature of knowing that you are everything you possibly can be. The bigger you become, the more complicated your life can become. Living BIG can cause blockage in your mind due to thinking too much of yourself. Always remain humble. Patrick Willis, a great friend of mine and a retired linebacker of the San Francisco 49ers says, *"I remained humble during my NFL career, but I also stayed hungry."* The lack of humility in response to God's spirit in your life and the lack of thirst can add to your complexity. Complexity is a clog in your energy channels. You simplify your life when you accept that you, and you alone, are responsible for the quality of your life. That notion alone should be enough to make you humble in the presence of God's grace. Superman is not coming; Wonder Woman isn't either. Only you have the power to control the quality of your human experiences. Only you have the power to create your

AMAZINGLY RIDICULOUS life. Switch your Power On, and Be BIG!

Our mind is the reservoir in which we contain our many thoughts, impulses, emotions, reactions, mental perceptions, instincts, and memories. What is within this mass core of consciousness and unconsciousness is dormant until we provide a spark that energizes its power. We can switch the power on and set our souls on fire. We can become a burning inferno that empowers us to take purposeful and unapologetic control of our lives and transform ourselves into the being of our own making. There is a massive river of flammable liquid that runs through our reservoir of emotions, thoughts, and perceptions. The river of fuel must be set on fire if our lives are to become amazing. This burning flame can jump-start the soul, rekindle the imagination, and rejuvenate that which has gone dormant in us. When the soul is on fire, the natural limitations of the human psyche are modified, and our supernatural abilities can now come out and play. You can now be BIG! You don't have to play yourself small. You can set your soul ablaze and turn the power on any time you put your mind to it. In fact, only by sparking the flames in ourselves are we able to truly cope with the travails of life and grow toward the light. So it is all on you. The fuel is already inside, and your thoughts are the spark. Send a spark into the reservoir. Your life awaits. Be Brilliant! Be Independent! Be Grand! Be BIG! Switch your power on and turn your energy up to the highest level, and rip off the knob. Today your AMAZINGLY RIDICULOUS life begins.

Dream Big Dreams

To DREAM is to Desire, Resolve, Excel, Achieve, and Move. To be BIG is to be Brilliant, Independent, and Gigantic. To DREAM BIG means to desire, resolve, excel, achieve and move in a brilliant, independent, and gigantic manner to create a wonderful, amazing, and ridiculous vision for your life. So Dream Big! I have always had dreams. I had many dreams of becoming a big-time music producer, lyricist, and songwriter. I even thought I was on my way when I was working with some up-and-coming hip hop artists in Atlanta. Because of some unforeseen circumstances and just some bad human traits that one can encounter in the music industry, music did not work out for me; even though it could still happen. I still have dreams, but I know the very moment that my dreams got really big.

That moment was when I met Dr. Michael Chitwood, founder and CEO of ICCM World Ministries and the firm Chitwood & Chitwood. Chitwood & Chitwood is the oldest and largest firm in the world specializing in providing financial services for churches, ministries, and non-profit organizations. I am a minister at ICCM in Chattanooga, TN. One day I was walking out of the church facility and Dr. Chitwood said, "Son, I want you to come sit in my car." My wife, Erica, and I gladly slid right into Dr. Chitwood's car, a laid-out Rolls Royce! Dr. Chitwood then said, "Son, God is waiting to bless you!" I had never before sat in a Rolls. This was just one of the many ways that Dr. Chitwood, from the very moment I met him, has encouraged me to think bigger and open my imagination up to much bigger dreams. Because of Dr. Chitwood and the love he and his family have shown me, my wife, and our family, I am dreaming bigger. And because of Ron Hickey I understand what it takes to rise to my ZENITH and live there.

Dr. Chitwood and Ron Hickey have invested heavily in my life. There have been many over the years who have poured inspiration, hope, and dreams into me. My father left me with so much wisdom, and my mother motivates me in her own way, despite their lives. My wife Erica is my rock and my children are the reason I do all that I do to come up in this world. I dream big so my children can dream big. One of my biggest motivators is Pastor Jeffrey Seay. Pastor Jeffrey encourages me daily to rise to my highest level. My family and friends from East Bakewell, TN and around the world have invested heavily in my life, and my best friend Joe Ervin and his wife have been and remain my greatest fans. They are believers in me. Joe tells me constantly, "Reece, I believe in you! I just want to be there when it happens!" Everyone can dream bigger dreams, be ridiculous and live an amazing life. I am blessed with an amazing support system, some natural God-given talent, and the commitment to the 19 RIDICULOUS HABITS necessary to live an amazing life. But it all starts with my big dreams. What are your big dreams? Are your dreams big enough?

To DREAM BIG you must:

DREAM

Desire a wonderful, amazing, and ridiculous life;
Resolve to make your desires a reality, no matter what;
Excel quickly around, over and under your limits;
Achieve to your fullest potential with all your might;
Move boldly beyond your current circumstances;

BIG

Brilliant–be brilliantly smart enough to make your dreams come true;
Independent–be independent in your thoughts and your actions; and
Gigantic–be gigantic in your imagination of what you can become in life.

DREAM–Desire, Resolve, Excel, Achieve, and Move

You must **Desire** a wonderful, amazing, and ridiculous life. That is the very first step to making your dreams come true. Desire creates the passion that you must have if you plan to travel to great destinations in your life. Passion fuels the soul, and when you ignite the fuel it sets your entire soul on fire. Desire is the fire that gives your life the energy to transform itself. Without energy nothing is possible. But desire alone is not enough. You must also have discipline, and you must be committed. Today is your beginning, and the time of any new beginning is precious, but fragile. You must first commit to the journey ahead and develop great discipline toward the things you desire. Discipline sustains your commitment, and commitment focuses your time and energy. To transform your life, your energy must be focused; and this level of focus requires great discipline. Life is an interesting proposition. It pushes and pulls you into many directions. Circumstances and conditions change all the time. So you can be easily tempted to waste your precious life energy on any of a plethora of ideas, thoughts, situations, or enticements that come your way. You can't chase a thousand ideas. You can't move into every situation. You can't entertain every single thought that enters your mind. You can't indulge each enticing moment in your life. That's why commitment and discipline toward the right desires are the two most critical elements in living the life you desire. Without such a commitment and discipline in regards to the things you most chiefly desire, you simply waste time and energy, and the life you desire never comes true. So desire a wonderful, amazing, and ridiculous life and develop the discipline and commitment and watch how your life begins to flourish.

You must **Resolve** to make your desires a reality, no matter what. Make a commitment today—on the very spot you are standing, sitting, or lying on. You must not stumble or hesitate in your actions to make your desires a reality. Create your own path, your own destiny, if necessary. Your resolve to self-determine what your life becomes is your greatest attribute. Without such dogged-determination you will be unable to navigate through life. Adversity is a guarantee, as well as struggle; but do not give up, no matter what! Keep going, irrespective of circumstance, and allow your AMAZINGLY RIDICULOUS imagination to help you push through when things become overwhelmingly tough. You will make it, as long as you keep charging forward. If you can't fly, drive. If you can't drive, run. If you can't run, walk. If you can't walk, crawl. If you can't crawl, ask someone to carry you (you will need help at times). Whatever happens, resolve to keep moving. You must learn to overcome your failures, frustrations, and fears. You must stay the course. Unhappiness, discomfort, and obstacles will come your way. You will experience pain and disappointments. That's life, and life is not a fairytale. Accept that, and keep moving. Abandon any rescue fantasies you may have. If there is a superman, he is in you. If there is a superwoman, she is in you. All you have is this life. Dream big and make the best of it. With each day, you have the opportunity to prove that you are the chosen one. Your time here in this life is short-lived and precious. Treasure every moment, dream big and resolve to make your desires your reality and have an AMAZINGLY RIDICULOUS life.

You must **Excel** quickly around, over and under your self-imposed limits. Life is an obstacle course that you must learn to navigate with speed, agility, toughness, and endurance. Yes, you must excel through life as if you were an athlete running the gauntlet. Whatever is in your path resisting your forward progress, you must quickly get around it, over it, or under it. Your limits, your obstacles, are self-imposed. Even when someone else places something in your path, you must agree to allow it to stand in your way. You must accept an object or situation as an obstacle before it can actually become one. So, as an athlete of life, you must develop a warrior's mentality and yield to nothing and no one. When you see obstacles ahead, quickly decide how you will get around, over or under. Commit to the decision and move with God's speed, emotional agility, mental toughness, and spiritual endurance. Be strong in your every conviction and let your actions be resolute. Whatever you have chosen as an occupation—whether you are a nurse, police officer, firefighter, doctor, lawyer, athlete, writer, salesperson, real estate agent, or any one of a number of other vocations in life—you have to compete. Therefore preparation, positioning, and awareness are also very critical to expeditiously moving past your obstacles. You excel when you are prepared. You excel when you are positioned. You excel when you are aware. Preparation, positioning, and awareness allow you to transcend your emotional limits and transform your thoughts into actions that allow you to conquer your self-imposed limits. While your big dreams require you to be unyielding to the competition in your pursuit of an AMAZINGLY

RIDICULOUS life, be compassionate at all times. In life we fall down and someone has to help us get up, and your compassion will determine who bends down to lend a helping hand. This is why being a compassionate warrior is the best way to make your big dreams come true. You must be quick, versatile, tough, and able to endure to get around, over and under your obstacles; but be kind to others as you run your obstacle course.

You must **Achieve** to your fullest potential with all your might. Everyone wishes to reach great levels of achievement in life, but life comes with its difficulties. Dreaming big pushes you past those difficulties with a resounding cheer. Big dreams increase your determination. Without determination, life can tear your down and push you into a valley. For that reason, all of your might, all of your strength, is required to achieve to your fullest potential. When confronted with life's challenges, big dreamers respond with exaltation and grandiosity. Big dreamers refuse to stay down. You have somewhere to get to when you have big dreams, and you don't let anything stop you. When things are tough and achieving at a high level becomes a struggle, you have to concentrate and focus your resources and energy. You have to summon your inner-being and force your will upon the circumstances that are pulling you down and not go quietly into the valley of despair. Achieving to your fullest potential oftentimes requires you to closely examine the situation and use all of your energy in a concentrated effort to achieve one great thing before you can get on with the rest of your life. Have you ever had a big exam, or an important job interview? Perhaps, it was a newborn baby or a suddenly unexpected tragedy in life; or it could be something as simple as a flat tire or a knot in your necklace. Whatever the case, when striving to make your big dreams come true, a concentration of your energy, an examination of the situation, and a summoning of your greatest might is required to achieve your fullest potential and live your wonderful, amazing, and ridiculous life.

You must **Move** boldly beyond your current circumstances. When you put distance between yourself and your circumstances, your circumstances cannot hinder you. The farther you move beyond the current circumstances that are holding you back, the less impact or harm those circumstances have on your life. If you are in a bad relationship, move beyond that relationship. If you are working at a dead-end job, move beyond that job. If your family and people around your tear you down and tell you that you will amount to nothing, move beyond them. Put distance between yourself and those things that add nothing of value to your life. It's hard to dream big when you can't see past your current bad situation. Sometimes a new zip code, a new job, a new relationship, a new environment, or a new attitude is the very thing your life needs. It may seem to make only a small difference at first. That's because you are comparing yourself to others, and you are not asking yourself what the possibilities are. Sometimes it is difficult to see the good life because of the all the trash that has been dumped on your doorstep. Start walking until you can no longer see the doorstep and never turn back. You don't have to have a destination in mind initially. Just get to a place where your mind can relax and your soul is at ease. Then contemplate the road ahead. Moving beyond your current circumstances means getting to a place where no one can hinder you or take anything of value from you. Moving beyond your current circumstances means deciding that you will no longer be someone else's punching bag or the object of their ridicule. It means getting to a place where no one else has access. Such a place can protect you, sustain, and guide you. It's amazing what life can become when you reach an oasis of protection, sustenance, and guidance. And if your current circumstances do not provide those things, move boldly beyond that situation. If you do not know how far to walk or how much distance there should be between you and the things that are holding you back from having a wonderful, amazing, and ridiculous life, then just keep moving until your heart is content. Once you get there, indulge a little in your contentment and delight in the joy of what you now see; then keep moving boldly toward the life you dream of. Remember: Stay in constant motion, and travel every day to the very edge of what you know.

Be BIG–Brilliant, Independent and Gigantic

Be **Brilliant**–smart enough to make your dreams come true. Everyone wants to be brilliant; brilliantly smart is even better. You, and you alone, must have the knowledge, skill, intelligence, and smartness—the brilliance to make your big dreams come true. In fact, no one can do it but you. Brilliance brings clarity of mind, clarity of spiritual teachings, and clarity of intellectual writing. Brilliance brings us fortune and happiness, and makes us joyously content. When we have brilliance, we are able to live a wonderful, amazing, and ridiculous life. When you are brilliant and your mind is clear of confusion and contention, joy and sadness become the same things to you because you move mentally beyond the temporary ups and downs of life. You understand nothing is permanent in this world. There is no such thing as everlasting on earth. Life is in constant transition, and where you end up is solely up to you. True brilliance goes far beyond simple intellectual capacity, more than just being book smart or experience wise. Being brilliant means going to the very edge of what you think you know and connecting to other possibilities. It's very possible to be very happy in life. It's highly possible that you will be highly successful. There's a possibility that your big dreams will come true. You see these possibilities and others when you travel to edge of your knowledge and look out into the open space. Many remain at the center of their knowledge because it feels safer and more secure, and as a result, never approach the edges of brilliance. But for those who are really seeking to live life more abundantly, then here's the entry point. You have to decide if you want to jump in or not. Brilliance comes from focusing all your human faculties into a single point; that point being your unique perception. Your perception is what you see in life. It is also the sounds you make and the sounds you hear. If you connect your vision to the sounds, you will generate an energy that will illuminate your path on this journey. That illumination is the concentrated power of your mind. The force of your mind's power will reveal your truth in this life. Your truth is your brilliance. Your brilliance is the inner-energy that allows you to self-determine what your life will become. Be Brilliant! Be BIG!

Be **Independent**—in your thoughts and in your actions. Life sometimes requires that we go at it alone. As humans, we naturally want to travel with others, but there are times when we serve ourselves and others better by being independent in our thoughts and actions. Get to where you are going first and then send for others. We come into this life as individuals, and we live as individuals; and most of the space in between finds us standing alone, metaphorically. We have to live our own lives. No one can do it for us. We are here, with our God-given volition, to self-liberate the anecdote. That is, to take it upon ourselves to write our story and have that story read exactly how we would want it to read. We get to write our narrative independent of what others would have us say. Everyone has their own golden pen, and our life is the journal we write. We are the authors of the manuscripts we are acting out. We get to make our character in our story be as flamboyant, grandiose, and brilliant as we decide. We are here to grab life by the edges and make of it what we will. Nothing before us or after us really matters. While it is a good thing to take the past and future into consideration, we have to be who we are, like the lilies in the field, independent of other beings. While we try to live in harmony with others and the universe, we must first make ourselves as wonderful, amazing, and ridiculous as we can. If we all can do just that, what a wonderful, amazing, and ridiculous life we all could live; independently and harmoniously at the same time. Be Independent! Be BIG!

Be **Gigantic**–in your imagination of what you can become in life. How do you measure yourself? How do you measure other people and other things? How do other people and other things measure you? Have you ever stopped to think of how something in nature—such as a lion, giraffe, tree or mountain—measures itself? We tend to measure ourselves by our physical height, weight, genital size, breast size, feet, hands, etc. We also measure how fast we can run, what college we attended, the size of our bank account, etc. What is really interesting is no matter how we measure ourselves, we never really measure up to anything in nature. We have never built anything as large as a mountain. We have never created anything as majestic as a tree or as graceful as a lion. Giraffes have 50 pound hearts. Wow! We built the pyramids in Egypt, the Great Wall of China, and the Empire State Building. While these man-made monuments are large in size and scope, they are unimportant to human vitality. They are categorically unnecessary things. We have used our imagination to build some enormous things in this life—from universities to Silicon Valley, from freeways to space travel, from box cars to artificial intelligence. But we do very little to increase the size of our human nature. We work all day and at the end have done next to nothing to give a gigantic boost to our minds or our souls. As humans, we have great imaginations. We use these great imaginations to create social media platforms, Androids and iPhones, and all sorts of artificial things; but we seldom use our imaginations to create a better way of being human. We don't use our imagination for building a better process for making our big dreams come true so we can live a wonderful, amazing, and ridiculous life. If we can somehow begin to more deeply contemplate, what more can we possibly become in this life? We will realize what the world needs more than anything are imaginations that re-imagine us as better humans. Our gigantic imaginations can make us happier, healthier, and friendlier. Can you imagine your human nature being as large as a mountain, as majestic as a tree, or as graceful as a lion? Can you imagine your life being wonderful, amazing, and ridiculous? Your imagination can create the reality you dream of. Be Gigantic! Be BIG!

52 WEEKLY QUOTES

Inspiring, Empowering, Motivating, and Thought Provoking Quotes on Dreams and Success

1. "All men dream: but not equally. Those who dream by night in the dusty recesses of their minds wake in the day to find that it was vanity: but the dreamers of the day are dangerous men, for they may act their dreams with open eyes, to make it possible."

– T.E. Lawrence

2. "Start where you are. Use what you have. Do what you can."
– Arthur Ashe

3. "The only thing that will stop you from fulfilling your dreams is you."
– Tom Bradley

4. "You see things; and you say, 'Why?' But I dream things that never were; and I say, 'Why not?'"

– George Bernard Shaw

5. "Life is full of beauty. Notice it. Notice the bumble bee, the small child, and the smiling faces. Smell the rain, and feel the wind. Live your life to the fullest potential, and fight for your dreams."

– Ashley Smith

6. "It doesn't matter where you're from, your dreams are valid."

— Lupita Nyong'o

7. "You are never too old to set another goal or to dream a new dream."

— C.S. Lewis

8. "What you do not started today you never finished tomorrow."

— Johann Wolfgang von Goethe

9. "Like success, failure is many things to many people. With positive mental attitude, failure is a learning experience, a rung on the ladder, and a plateau at which to get your thoughts in order to prepare to try again."

— W. Clement Stone

10. "Do not follow where the path may lead. Go instead where there is no path and leave a trail."

— Ralph Waldo Emerson

11. "Dream as if you'll live forever, live as if you'll die today."

— James Dean

12. "Ever tried. Ever failed. No matter. Try Again. Fail again. Fail better."

— Samuel Beckett

13. "There are some people who live in a dream world, and there are some who face reality; and then there are those who turn one into the other."

— Douglas H. Everett

14. "Never limit yourself because of others' limited imagination; never limit others because of your own limited imagination."

— Mae Jemison

15. "A dreamer is one who can only find his way by moonlight, and his punishment is that he sees the dawn before the rest of the world."

— Oscar Wilde

16. "You are always right about yourself. If you say you can, you can. If you say you can't, you can't."

— Ronald T. Hickey

17. "Hold fast to dreams for if dreams die, life is a broken-winged bird that cannot fly."

— Langston Hughes

18. "Do not be embarrassed by your failures, learn from them and start again."

— Richard Branson

19. "Keep away from people who try to belittle your ambitions. Small people always do that, but the really great make you feel that you, too, can become great."

– Mark Twain

20. "Dream no small dreams for they have no power to move the hearts of men."

– Johann Wolfgang von Goethe

21. "It is not a disaster to be unable to capture your ideal, but it is a disaster to have no ideal to capture." It is not a disgrace not to reach the stars, but it is a disgrace to have no stars to reach for. Not failure, but low aim is sin."

– Benjamin E. Mays

22. "To accomplish great things, we must not only act, but also dream; not only plan, but also believe."

– Anatole France

23. "When I'm old and dying, I plan to look back on my life and say, 'Wow, that was an adventure,' not, 'Wow, I sure felt safe.'"

– Tom Preston-Werner

24. "There is only one thing that makes a dream impossible to achieve: the fear of failure."

– Paulo Coelho

25. "If you are not willing to risk the usual, you will have to settle for the ordinary."

– Jim Rohn

26. "The key to realizing a dream is to focus not on success but significance – and then even the small steps and little victories along your path will take on greater meaning."

– Oprah Winfrey

27. "Never give up on a dream just because of the time it will take to accomplish it. The time will pass anyway."

– Earl Nightingale

28. "Go confidently in the direction of your dreams. Live the life you have imagined."

– Henry David Thoreau

29. "I have spread my dreams beneath your feet; Tread softly because you tread on my dreams."

– William Butler Yeats

30. "The best years of your life are the ones in which you decide your problems are your own. You do not blame them on your mother, the ecology, or the president. You realize that you control your own destiny."

– Albert Ellis

31. "Of all forms of caution, caution in love is perhaps the most fatal to true happiness."

– Bertrand Russell

32. "Nothing in the world can take the place of perseverance. Talent will not; nothing is more common than unsuccessful people with talent. Genius will not; unrewarded genius is almost legendary. Education will not; the world is full of educated derelicts. Perseverance and determination alone are omnipotent."

– Calvin Coolidge

33. "It is only when we truly know and understand that we have a limited time on earth – and that we have no way of knowing when our time is up – that we will begin to live each day to the fullest, as if it was the only one we had."
– Elizabeth Kubler-Ross

34. "So many of our dreams at first seem impossible, then they seem improbable, and then, when we summon the will, they soon become inevitable."

– Christopher Reeve

35. "If you have built castles in the air, your work need not be lost; that is where they should be. Now put the foundation under them."

– Henry David Thoreau

36. "If you take responsibility for yourself you will develop a hunger to accomplish your dreams."

– Les Brown

37. "I have had dreams, and I've had nightmares. I overcame the nightmares because of my dreams."

– Jonas Salk

38. "It may be that those who do most, dream most."

– Stephen Butler Leacock

39. "Much of the stress that people feel doesn't come from having too much to do. It comes from not finishing what they started."

– David Allen

40. "If one advances confidently in the direction of one's dreams, and endeavors to live the life which one has imagined, one will meet with a success unexpected in common hours."

– Henry David Thoreau

41. "Whatever you do, or dream you can, begin it. Boldness has genius and power and magic in it."

– Johann Wolfgang von Goethe

42. "Amateurs sit and wait for inspiration, the rest of us just get up and go to work."

– Stephen King

43. "Be miserable. Or motivate yourself. Whatever has to be done, it's always your choice."

– Wayne Dyer

44. "You don't have to see the whole staircase, just take the first step."

– Martin Luther King, Jr.

45. "Do not spoil what you have by desiring what you have not; remember that what you now have was once among the things you only hoped for."

– Epicurus

46. "The most important first step to living the life of your dreams is this: Believe your dreams will come true and that you alone have the power to make them come true."

– Maurice Willis

47. "A dream doesn't become reality through magic; it takes sweat, determination, and hard work."

– Colin Powell

48. "The future belongs to those who believe in the beauty of their dreams."

— Eleanor Roosevelt

49. "Dreams do come true. Without that possibility, nature would not incite us to have them."

— John Updike

50. "The only thing worse than starting something and failing ... is not starting something."

— Seth Godin

51. "Dreaming is the essence of who you are. When you dare to dream, you lose yourself just long enough to learn who you really are."

— Ronald T. Hickey

52. "Every great dream begins with a dreamer. Always remember, you have within you the strength, the patience, and the passion to reach for the stars to change the world."

— Harriet Tubman